The New York Public Library Amazing African American History

A Book of Answers for Kids

Diane Patrick

A Stonesong Press Book

John Wiley & Sons, Inc.

New York • Chichester • Weinheim • Brisbane • Singapore • Toronto

12.95

Copyright ©1998 by The New York Public Library and The Stonesong Press, Inc.
Published by John Wiley & Sons, Inc.

Library of Congress Cataloguing-in-Publication Data

Patrick, Diane.
    The New York Public Library amazing African American history/
Diane Patrick.
        p.   cm. — (New York Public Library answer books for kids series)
    "A Stonesong Press book."
    Includes bibliographical references and index.
    Summary: Presents questions and answers relating to important periods in
African American history including the Revolution, Civil War, Reconstruction,
Migration, and the Civil Rights Movement.
    ISBN 0-471-19217-1 (pbk. : alk. paper)
    1. Afro-Americans—History—Miscellanea—Juvenile literature.
2. Questions and answers—Juvenile literature. [1. Afro-Americans—Miscellanea. 2.
Questions and answers.] I. Series.
E185.P34   1998
973' .0496073—dc21   97-16938
                                                            CIP

CONTENTS

INTRODUCTION

What was the price of slaves? What was the Montgomery bus boycott? Who were W. E. B. Du Bois, Phillis Wheatley, and Marcus Garvey?

These are just a few of the thousands of questions we might ask about our African American heritage. Now you can have the answers to some of these questions at your fingertips in **The New York Public Library Amazing African American History.**

The New York Public Library Amazing African American History doesn't include every detail—no one book could! But within these pages are the answers to questions about many of the most important events in African American history and some of the people who helped make it.

Some of the questions can only be answered with more questions; others may make you curious about an exciting part of history you never knew about before. Take the next step to knowledge: Research ideas and subjects interesting to you and come to your own conclusions. The New York Public Library and other public, school, and private libraries all over the country have shelves and computers filled with facts to help you learn. The librarians know what material they have and can help you find what you want. It is our hope that this book will encourage you to investigate our nation's African American heritage and to use the libraries in your own town.

FROM AFRICA TO COLONIAL AMERICA

What is slavery? ◆ When and where did slavery begin? ◆ What other countries were involved in the slave trade? ◆ When did the first black African come to America? ◆ What was an indentured servant? ◆ How did slavery develop in colonial America? ◆ When did slavery become legal in colonial America? ◆ Where did African slaves come from? ◆ What was Africa like before the Atlantic slave trade began? ◆ How were Africans captured for slavery? ◆ How did the captured Africans get to the United States? ◆ What was the voyage

What is slavery?

Slavery is the practice in which people are treated as property. A slave is owned by a master, made to do work for no pay, and can be sold or traded to someone else at any time.

When and where did slavery begin?

Human slavery began in prehistoric times. Originally, it had nothing to do with race: It was a system of using prisoners of war as servants or laborers for those who had captured them. Other slaves were criminals or people who could not pay their debts. Ancient Greeks, Romans, Africans, and Egyptians enslaved whomever they conquered. In early European cultures, slaves were servants owned by rich people. In the early 1500s, the Atlantic slave trade began when Spanish and Portuguese ships began transporting African slaves to the West Indies.

What other countries were involved in the slave trade?

By the end of the sixteenth century, Holland had become the leading African slave trader, followed by England and France after 1700. In the 1800s, the Danes, Swedes, and Germans all participated in the slave trade.

Early Explorers

Although no one knows for sure when the first Africans came to what is now the continental United States, there is solid evidence of some early black explorers in the area.

One of Christopher Columbus' companions on his voyage in 1492 was Pedro Alonzo Niño, a man who appears to have been of African descent. Another African man named Estevanico accompanied the Spanish explorers Panfilo de Narvaez and Alvar Nuñez de Vaca in explorations through what is now Arizona and New Mexico during the 1500s. Many other European explorers—including Vasco Nuñez de Balboa, Francisco Pizarro, and Hernán Cortés—counted blacks among their companions during their adventures.

When did the first black Africans come to colonial America?

The first known Africans to inhabit this region were a group of about twenty who arrived in Jamestown, Virginia, in 1619, on a Dutch ship with the English colonists. They were believed to be indentured servants, not slaves.

What was an indentured servant?

An indentured servant was any person, white or black, who worked as a servant under a contractlike arrangement for a set period of time—usually seven years. When that time was up, they were given a small amount of money, clothing, or plots of land to assist their transition to freedom.

How did slavery develop in colonial America?

Colonial America itself began in 1607 when Englishmen set up a **colony** (a settlement started by a government in another country) at Jamestown, Virginia, followed by others on the eastern coast of North America. Under the king's rule, these colonies were still considered to be a part of England (also known as Great Britain). By the middle of the 1700s, there were thirteen English colonies in America.

The early colonies needed money to survive. One of the ways the colonists earned money was by growing crops such as rice, cotton, tobacco, and indigo. These crops were sold primarily to England, as well as to other colonies. In order to grow more crops for sale, the colonists needed a steady supply of labor.

The American colonists originally used Native Americans and white indentured servants to do the work on the farms and **plantations** where the crops were grown. As time passed, the colonies, starting with Virginia, needed more workers. They soon heard that slave labor was helping Brazilian and Caribbean sugar plantation owners grow richer. As a result, the American colonists thought it would be a good idea to try that method themselves. Between 1700 and 1850, the demand for slaves rose greatly.

In Defense of Black Slavery

Clergymen in favor of slavery found passages in the Bible that they believed supported slavery. The most frequently used was Genesis 9:25–27. In these passages, Noah, upset by the misbehavior of his son Ham, who was thought to be black, cursed all the descendants of Ham's son Canaan. The curse was that they would be slaves forever, serving the rest of the population.

When did slavery become legal in colonial America?

Virginia made slavery legal in 1661 and passed a law the following year that stated that children born to a slave mother would also be slaves. During the 1600s, slavery based on race slowly became a way of life throughout all thirteen American colonies. By the beginning of the 1700s, new laws had been created that completely barred Africans and their descendants from enjoying the political rights and economic opportunities that whites enjoyed.

By the 1690s, about 10,000 slaves a year were shipped to the American colonies.

Where did African slaves come from?

Slaves were taken from hundreds of African villages and towns on the west coast of Africa and central Africa. By the late 1700s, there were also some taken from southern and eastern Africa. They came from many ethnic groups: Ashanti, Ibo, Hausa, Yoruba, Mandingo, and dozens more.

What was Africa like before the Atlantic slave trade began?

Long before European slavery, there were powerful, wealthy kingdoms in West Africa. Among them were ancient

An old map of Africa depicts the coast where Europeans traded for slaves. Some of the African kingdoms are noted.

Ghana, Mali, and Songhai (sometimes spelled Songhay), which flourished between the eighth and sixteenth centuries. They were located in the western Sudan, where the nations of Niger, Mauritania, Burkina Faso, and Mali stand now. Their wealth came from their gold, which they traded to other African and European countries. The Songhai kingdom was the largest and most important. Its city of Timbuktu, which still stands at the edge of the Sahara, was one of the world's greatest cities in the fifteenth and sixteenth centuries, a center of culture and learning. Law and medicine were taught at Timbuktu's great mosque of Sankore, and students came from all over to attend. Djenne (sometimes spelled Jenne) was another respected Songhai city. Beginning in the eighth century, Ghana dominated the Sudan for almost 300 years until it fell to a group of Muslim invaders and was succeeded by Mali. Mali had its heyday between the thirteenth and fifteenth centuries, and its place was taken by Songhai in the fifteenth and sixteenth centuries.

Africans in Africa

Many West Africans were skilled farmers and artists. In South Carolina, where slaves became a majority of the population, planters sought slaves from particular regions of Africa who possessed desired skills, such as the knowledge of rice cultivation, boat building, or coastal navigation. Some tribes made textiles and baskets; others worked with animal skins and furs and made clothing, weapons, and utensils. Still others worked with iron, copper, and precious stones.

The Songhai empire fell by the seventeenth century, after Songhai was invaded by North Africans from Morocco.

What was life like in the African homeland?

In this land of tropical forests, vast deserts, and grasslands, many societies were matrilineal; this means that inheritance and property rights descended through the mother. When a man and woman married, the groom left his family to join his bride's clan.

West Africans believed that spirits were all around them—living in rivers, rocks, animals, and forests. They treated nature with respect, awe, and extreme care. They also worshipped their ancestors, as they were considered the bridge between the supreme creator and the earth's inhabitants.

Much of the ceremonial sculpture, metalwork, and jewelry produced in sixteenth-century West Africa was skillfully crafted and elaborate, showing a very high level of artistic development.

How were Africans captured for slavery?

Some were prisoners of African tribal and national wars. Slave traders formed trading companies and set up trading stations (known as forts) in areas where they wanted to obtain slaves. Representatives of the companies went to do business with the local chiefs. By plying the chiefs with various trade goods, trinkets, and liquor, the traders convinced them to sell the prisoners of war as slaves.

Most slaves were taken from coastal areas such as Angola, Senegambia, and the region bordering the Bights of Benin and Biafra.

Slaves were routinely branded with a hot iron to designate which company acquired them.

Other Africans were kidnapped from their villages. The traders themselves did not capture the slaves; using the promise of European goods, they encouraged the Africans to raid one another's villages, seize whatever captives they could, and march them to the trading stations.

How did the captured Africans get to the Americas?

Captured Africans were taken to the forts and held until there were enough Africans to fill up a ship. The captives were loaded onto slave ships for the trip across the Atlantic Ocean. Most were taken to the West Indies or South America, but about half a million were brought directly to North America.

Today, on Goree Island near Senegal, a ruin of a slave-trading fort still stands.

What was the voyage across the Atlantic like?

The ocean voyage from Africa to colonial America or the West Indies lasted between five and twelve weeks, and was known as the **Middle Passage** because it was the middle leg of the slave ship's three-part trip: from the ship's country of origin to Africa, then from Africa to the West Indies, then from the West Indies back to the country of origin. The slave ships were usually sloops (one-masted vessels) or schooners (two-masted vessels) that held fifty to one hundred tons.

The ships typically carried a crew of eight to fifteen men plus the captain. On some ships, the available space below was made into several decks, which were completely filled with slaves crammed together as tightly as possible, lying on their backs with their hands and feet chained. Each deck was approximately three feet in height, so that there was no room for the Africans to move or to sit up.

Men, women, and children were kept in separate areas. Conditions were filthy, with dysentery, smallpox, and other diseases a constant problem. On some ships,

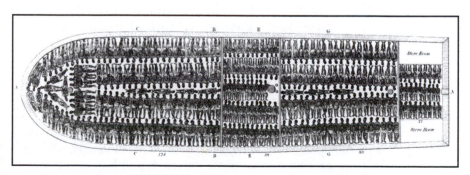

During the Middle Passage, slaves were crammed together as tightly as possible, forced to lie on their backs with their hands and feet chained.

An estimated one in every seven captives died during the Middle Passage.

captives saw daylight only when they were taken on deck for exercise—that is, being forced by a whip to "dance."

Did any Africans die during the voyage?

The extremely unsanitary conditions at sea inevitably caused violent sickness. Because of rampant illness, violence, suicide, and murder, many of the captives—an estimated one to two million—did not survive these cruel voyages. Many others arrived psychologically damaged or near death.

How were slaves bought and sold in North America?

Slaves were bought and sold at slave markets and auctions, which were held in public. Most auctions were held at the county courthouse. There, licensed traders, who represented the seller or the buyer, would buy or sell slaves. They examined the slaves carefully, looking for whip scars (which meant that the slave might be unruly) and checking teeth for signs of age. The auctioneer would provide additional information, such as a female's ability to bear children or a male's ability to perform heavy labor. Slaves were also purchased and sold in private agreements between buyer and seller.

What was the price of slaves?

In the 1600s, slaves were bought in Africa for about $25 or its equivalent in goods. They were sold in the colonies for about $150 each. The price depended on their condition, age, abilities, and—in the case of women—their ability to have children. In the early 1800s, the prices of prime **field hands** ranged from $350 in Virginia to about $500 in Louisiana. As the demand increased, the prices rose. By 1860, prime field hands were selling for about $1,000 in Virginia and $1,500 in New Orleans.

Were slave families kept together?

In Africa, the family was extremely important. Families might have hundreds of members and consist of several

African families were routinely broken up by the slave traders.

generations. But slave traders had no respect for African families. They would buy or sell a child, parent, or spouse whenever they wanted to, especially if the price was right. As a result, African families were routinely broken up by the slave trade.

How were the slaves paid for?

Slave traders paid for the Africans with either currency or products from Europe. In North and South America, they sold slaves for currency or commodities—such as tobacco, rice, sugar, and cotton—which were sold in Europe at a high profit.

What was life like for slaves in early colonial America?

Slaves could be bought and sold, and their families could be separated. They were usually not paid for their hard work, could not choose how to make a living, or decide where to live. At the whim of their owners, slaves could be beaten, imprisoned, tortured, or even killed if they "misbehaved."

How many slaves were there in the North American colonies?

According to the 1790 census—the first census taken in the new nation—there were 697,897 enslaved blacks in the original thirteen states.

Who owned slaves?

In the North and South, many slave owners were whites who owned small farms. Usually there were about twenty slaves on these farms. Other southern slave holders owned large plots of land, or plantations, on which they grew a crop that they sold.

What is a plantation?

A plantation is a large farm. In colonial America, plantations were found mostly in the southern colonies because they had the largest tracts of rich farmland. Plantations were often built alongside rivers, as it was faster and easier to ship goods by water than by land. The plantations needed many people to work the land, which is why plantation owners used slaves. Some plantations operated like small towns, each with a flour mill, a blacksmith, shoemakers, carpenters, and weavers all living and working there.

What kind of work did slaves do?

In the South, most slaves worked on cotton, tobacco, and rice plantations. Slaves also worked in Louisiana's salt mines, rope factories in Kentucky, the iron factories of Virginia, and the North Carolina cotton mills. In the North, the slaves worked in cities, on farms, and on ships.

On plantations, field slaves (or field hands, as they were also known) did the hardest and most physically exhausting work. For fifteen or sixteen hours every day, they raised crops, herded cattle, and slaughtered animals. On many cotton plantations, slaves were required to pick 250 pounds a day, and were frequently whipped if they picked less. After sundown, the slaves still had to perform other chores, such as cutting wood and feeding the animals, before they could return to their quarters.

On the next level in the slave hierarchy were house slaves and skilled slave laborers, who kept the master's household running smoothly. They lived in or near the "big house," where the master's family lived. Working as a house slave was considered an honor. House slaves wore uniforms or the white family's discarded clothing. The most important house slave was the butler, because he supervised all the male house servants. His wife usually supervised all the female house servants. Other house slaves included waiters, gardeners, and carriage drivers.

How were slaves controlled?

Virginia was the first colony to create slave codes, or laws, and the other colonies followed suit. These laws stated that slaves were property, not people, and could be sold at any time; that they could not marry, learn how to read or write, hold unauthorized religious services, or gather for any reason without permission. Slaves were also prohibited from suing or testifying in court, and were forbidden to strike a white person, even in self-defense. They could not

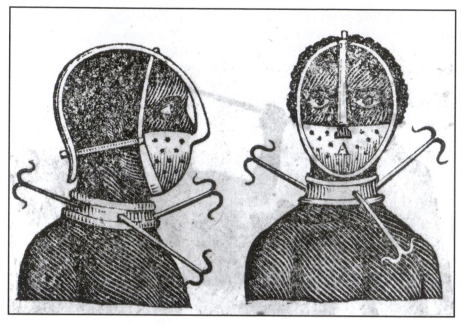

Cruel devices were sometimes used to control slaves.

leave the plantation without written permission, or visit—or be visited by—whites or free blacks.

These laws were enforced by county and state officers, called patrollers, who whipped and sometimes killed slaves caught on the road without their masters' written permission.

On plantations, the overseers used slave drivers to maintain discipline and make sure no slave idled or did bad work in the fields. Punishment—which was given for anything considered to be impudence—was given or supervised by the slavemaster or overseer. The most common punishment was thirty-nine lashes with a whip, but—depending on the personality of the person giving the punishment—could be more or less cruel.

Where did slaves live?

For field slave families, home was a small one- or two-room cabin where as many as twelve people might live. Archaeologists excavating seventeenth- and eighteenth-century sites found that slave dwellings in those early years of slavery had clay walls and thatch roofs, similar to those in West Africa. By the nineteenth century, log cabins were used as slave quarters.

The cabins were sweltering hot in summer and freezing cold in winter. Slaves made mattresses of straw or moss and were given thin cotton blankets. Their usual furniture was wooden benches and chairs. They used knives and wooden spoons provided by the slave owners, or made their own wooden utensils. They made bowls and jugs out of dried gourds.

What did slaves eat?

Typically, slaves were given very small amounts of food, which might include meat, flour, milk, lard, cornmeal, and greens. Throughout the South, their major staple was corn. Although rice was available, it was worth more, and so was saved for export (or sale abroad). Slaves ate corn with pork and beef and supplemented the meat they were given with wild fruits and nuts. Bones from turtles, fish, raccoons, rabbits, wild turkey, and deer have been found at slave archaeological sites.

What did slaves do after their work was finished?

At night, on Saturday afternoons, and on Sundays, most slaves were allowed to go hunting and fishing, do personal chores, work in their own gardens, and get together with other slaves. If they had a pass from their owner, they could visit friends on nearby plantations.

What happened when slaves got sick?

Most slaves treated themselves and other slaves and rarely saw white doctors. Slaves were quite successful in treating everything from coughs to backaches and snake bites with natural remedies, and many of these remedies were also sought by whites. Slave women acted as midwives, handling the birth of most of the babies born to

Enslaved Children

By age five or six, children would do small tasks such as helping in the big house or in the field fetching water, picking up stones, or working in the trash gang. At the age of ten or twelve, children—both boys and girls—were given a regular field routine.

Slaves and Healing

In the early eighteenth century, a slave taught Reverend Cotton Mather how to inject a patient with a small-pox vaccine, which was a serum made from a weaker form of the disease. A perfected version of that method is still used today to make vaccines for many illnesses, including the flu.

Another slave, known only as Cesar, created a cure for rattle-snake bites, which was published in the *South Carolina Gazette* in 1751. This accomplishment led the South Carolina General Assembly to grant his freedom.

Wilcie Elfe of Charleston, South Carolina, was a black pharmacist who had been trained by his owner, a doctor. Elfe later ran his own very successful practice; he even patented his drugs and sold them all over South Carolina.

Another slave, James Derham, served as a medical assistant to his slave owner, Dr. Robert Dove, eventually purchasing his freedom. Derham later set up his own practice.

David K. McDonough developed a national reputation when he served on staff at New York's Eye and Ear Infirmary during the eighteenth century.

---

slave mothers. Some of the men were spiritual leaders and often served as healers.

What religion did the Africans practice?

Africans were very religious. Many believed in a supreme god who created the earth. They also believed in ancestor worship, and that the spirit still existed after the death of the individual. About one-fifth of the enslaved Africans held Islamic beliefs.

When the Africans came to America, most of their religious practices were banned and they were exposed to Christianity. Still, the slaves created their own interpretations of white beliefs, combining a belief in Jesus with belief in spirits who could help the living. They added African rhythms, melodies, and patterns—such as the call and response—to standard Christian hymns and thus created spirituals of their own.

Were all black people in the colonies slaves?

Before slavery became official, a small population of free black men and women already lived in the North

American colonies. Many of these were indentured servants who had completed their service and were freed. Following their freedom, some began to accumulate money, property, and servants. Some slaves purchased their freedom with money earned on the side, and others were freed by owners who made provisions in their wills.

Did anyone protest slavery in early America?

Slavery was always controversial. Antonio Montesino and Bartolomé de las Casas, sixteenth-century Spanish missionaries in North America, were critical of slavery. In the seventeenth century, English and American Quakers opposed slavery and the slave trade. During the eighteenth century, British **abolitionists** (people who fought against slavery) spoke out against the slave trade, knowing that their country transported the greatest number of African slaves to the New World. In 1772, Granville Sharp, a humanitarian (someone who promotes the welfare of all humans), persuaded the British courts to declare that slavery could not exist in England.

By the 1780s, slavery was being attacked by religious leaders, economists, and political philosophers. In 1787, Thomas Clarkson, Granville Sharp, and Josiah Wedgwood (a famous English potter), formed a society for the abolition of the slave trade. Many sympathetic and dedicated whites of all backgrounds were very active in the abolitionist movement.

Were there any schools for blacks during the colonial period?

Elias Neau, a Frenchman, operated a school for African Americans in New York as early as 1704. The first blacks to be employed as teachers were named Harry and Andrew (last names unknown). They started a school for slaves in South Carolina, where they taught basic reading and writing. The first black school in U.S. history was the New York Free

Why Black Slaves?

In the colonists' opinion, Native Americans were not suited to be slaves because they caught European diseases too easily. Indentured servants were also unsuitable because there weren't enough of them and they were protected by law from being enslaved. Africans were used as slaves instead because they were strong, not protected by laws, and could be identified easily by their skin color if they tried to escape.

African School, created in 1787 by the New York Society for Promoting the Manumission of Slaves. In the eighteenth and nineteenth centuries, this was the most recognized independent school for African Americans.

How did colonial slaves obtain education?

Education was one of the first steps toward unlocking the chains of slavery—but it was against the law for a slave to be taught to read or write. Those who wanted to learn used the Bible, or depended on abolitionists and young white school children who considered it an adventure to teach slaves. They also relied on free blacks and white adults who secretly taught slaves in their homes or isolated places. The slaves stole books from the private libraries of the slaveholders and got help from other blacks who could read and write. Some could read and write well enough to forge valuable passes, giving them freedom to roam the countryside.

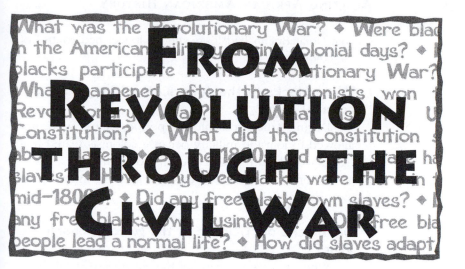

FROM REVOLUTION THROUGH THE CIVIL WAR

What was the Revolutionary War?

By the middle of the 1700s, the American colonists were very unhappy with the way they were being ruled by the English king. For example, the British had imposed heavy taxes that the colonists believed were unfair. When the colonists refused to pay, the British sent troops to harass them into paying the taxes. The colonists began to resist. Finally, on April 19, 1775, war broke out. This war, which lasted until 1781, was called the Revolutionary War (also known as the American Revolution). At the end of the

The Declaration of Independence

In 1776, the thirteen colonies voted to declare their independence from Great Britain. Thomas Jefferson put their declaration in writing. This document was called the Declaration of Independence, and was signed by fifty-six representatives of the colonies.

The Declaration of Independence is written in language that is easy to understand. It has three parts. The first part, the Preamble, is the most important. It states that "all Men are created equal" and have "inalienable rights," and expresses belief in democracy, or rule by the people. This was an unusual idea in those days, because most countries were ruled by kings.

The second part of the Declaration is a long list of complaints against Great Britain's King George III.

The final part of the Declaration states that because of the above, the colonies are, and shall be, free and independent and no longer loyal to the British crown.

war, Great Britain had lost—and no longer had control of the colonies.

Were blacks in the American military during colonial days?

During America's colonial period, blacks were not allowed to join the military because colonists feared that blacks would harm whites or even revolt if they were given guns. Some also believed that blacks were inferior and incapable of fighting.

Did blacks participate in the Revolutionary War?

When war came, many of the colonies, particularly in the North, allowed blacks to take up arms. Early black fighting men were not drafted or obligated by law to serve the country; they volunteered. Many blacks volunteered to join the **Continental army** (the colonists' army) because they believed that a free United States would also give

Black Patriots in the American Revolution

On March 5, 1770, an angry crowd gathered in the streets of Boston, Massachusetts, to protest the unfair taxes and laws in the American colonies. British soldiers rushed to control the crowd. Crispus Attucks, a black seaman and escaped slave, was the first to confront the British soldiers. When the soldiers retaliated, Crispus Attucks was also the first man to die. This confrontation is known as the Boston Massacre, and Crispus Attucks's death is considered the first casualty of the Revolution.

Lemuel Haynes was one of many black **minutemen** who helped defend Concord Bridge. Peter Salem, who had been granted his freedom to enlist, was presented to General George Washington for his feat of shooting a British major. Primas Black and Epheram Blackman, members of Ethan Allen's Green Mountain Boys, participated in the capture of Fort Ticonderoga. Salem Poor was given a special commendation for leadership and courage, making him the first acknowledged black military hero in American history. Other black freedom fighters were Barzillai Lew, Cuff Whittemore, Pomp Blackman, Caesar and John Ferrit (father and son), Prince Estabrook, and Samuel Craft.

them freedom. Other blacks joined the British, who offered freedom to all slaves who joined their armies. By the end of the war, nearly 5,000 free blacks had fought with the American army and roughly one thousand slaves had gained their freedom through the British. Blacks served as spies, infantrymen, laborers, cooks, and drivers.

In 1792, Congress passed a law allowing only free white men to serve in the American military.

What did black women do during the war?

Some of the first accounts of black participation in the American military appear in the memoirs of Lucy Terry Prince (1730–1821). Prince, considered to be the first African American poet, tells of black women who disguised themselves as men to fight against the British in the Revolutionary War.

Black women and white women often worked together during the war, taking care of the wounded on the battlefields and operating the farms, homes, and businesses left behind.

What happened after the colonists won the Revolutionary War?

In 1783, Great Britain and the colonies, which now called themselves the United States, signed a peace treaty. Delegates from each state then tried to set up a nation that would stand for freedom and democracy as no nation ever had. In May 1787, they met to plan this new government. On September 17, 1787, they approved the U.S. Constitution, the legal document that described, in seven articles, how the United States would be governed, which is still what we follow today.

What is the U.S. Constitution?

The Constitution, adopted in 1788, is the document that describes the government of the United States. The Constitution was written very carefully so that government policies could not be made by one person or group. The people knew that any government with too much power could be dangerous, like the British rule they had recently escaped.

The new system was called a federal system of government, meaning that power would be shared by a central government, called the federal government, and state governments. The power of both governments would come from the people. Under the new system, the most important governing responsibilities were making laws, interpreting laws, and carrying out the laws. The government of the United States was separated into three parts, or branches (the executive, legislative, and judicial branches), that handle these responsibilities. None of these branches is supposed to have more power than another.

Because the individual states and the people in them had so much power, slavery was able to operate freely. The federal government would not interfere in the running of the states. The Constitution did allow for future changes, called amendments.

What did the Constitution say about slaves?

The writers of the Constitution thought that it was more important to form a nation than to end slavery. They decided not to refer to slavery in the Constitution. This is why the original Constitution did not use the words "black," "Negro," "African," or "slave." However, in three places in the original Constitution, it is clear that they are being referred to.

In Article I, section 2, the Constitution said that states would be taxed according to their populations plus "three-fifths of all other persons." The phrase "all other persons" referred to blacks, and put that way meant that blacks were considered less than full human beings.

U.S. Slave Population in 1860

Alabama: 435,000	Mississippi: 437,000
Arkansas: 111,000	Missouri: 115,000
Delaware: 2,000	North Carolina: 331,000
Florida: 62,000	South Carolina: 402,000
Georgia: 462,000	Tennessee: 276,000
Kentucky: 225,000	Texas: 183,000
Louisiana: 332,000	Virginia: 491,000
Maryland: 87,000	

100 DOLLARS
REWARD!

Ranaway from the subscriber on the 27th of July, my Black Woman, named

EMILY,

Seventeen years of age, well grown, black color, has a whining voice. She took with her one dark calico and one blue and white dress, a red corded gingham bonnet; a white striped shawl and slippers. I will pay the above reward if taken near the Ohio river on the Kentucky side, or THREE HUNDRED DOLLARS, if taken in the State of Ohio, and delivered to me near Lewisburg, Mason County, Ky.   THO'S. H. WILLIAMS.
    August 4, 1853.

Poster advertising reward for capture of runaway slave.

The second reference was in Article I, section 9, which stated that the "importation of certain persons" (the slave trade) could be stopped after 1808, and that Congress could then put a tax on anyone brought into the United States as a slave.

The third reference to slaves was in Article IV, section 2. It said that anyone escaping from bondage into another state would not be released from their labor, but would be returned to the party to whom they owe their service. This meant that runaway slaves would have to be returned to their masters.

These clauses in the Constitution recognized the existence and legality of slavery without actually saying so. They were later eliminated by constitutional amendments.

In South Carolina, there were more slaves than white residents. Most of the slaves in the South were owned by about 385,000 people.

By the 1860 census, the number of slaves had grown to 3,953,700 (the total southern population was about 12 million).

By the 1800s, did every state have slaves?

By mid-1820, there were twenty-two states in the United States. Eleven allowed slavery, and were called slave states; the other eleven were called free states.

In 1820, Missouri asked to become a state. In Congress, Northerners and Southerners fought about whether Missouri would become a slave state or a free state. Each group had the same number of senators, and wanted Missouri's senators on their side.

In a compromise, Congress finally decided that Missouri should become a slave state and that the next state, Maine, should be a free state. This agreement, known as the **Missouri Compromise,** stated that slavery would be prohibited north of 36°30′ north latitude, the westward extension of Missouri's southern boundary.

By 1850, the United States had grown from twenty-four states to thirty states. Again, there were an equal number (fifteen) of slave states and free states. California wanted to become a free state. The **Compromise of 1850** said that California would become a free state; additionally, the Fugitive Slave Act of 1793 was amended to coerce citizens (under threat of fine or imprisonment) to assist in the return of runaway slaves.

As of 1860, the slave-holding areas were Alabama, Arkansas, Delaware, the District of Columbia, Florida, Georgia, Kentucky, Louisiana, Maryland, Mississippi, Missouri, North Carolina, South Carolina, Tennessee, Texas, and Virginia. The free states were Connecticut, Minnesota, Illinois, Indiana, Iowa, Maine, Massachusetts, Michigan, New Hampshire, New Jersey, New York, Ohio, Pennsylvania, Rhode Island, Vermont, and Wisconsin.

How many free blacks were there in the mid–1800s?

The 1860 census listed 488,070 free blacks in the United States. Some—children of a slave mother and a white slavemaster, for example—had been freed privately. Some had been slaves who had saved enough money, from outside work, to buy their freedom. Others had been given their freedom as a reward for faithful service or had been freed after their owner's death by a provision in the

Black Businesspeople of the 1800s

Paul Cuffe (1759–1817), a free black man, operated his own successful shipbuilding company in Connecticut in the late 1700s and early 1800s. He used the wealth he accumulated to help other blacks.

Former Mississippi slave William Johnson, freed in 1820, earned a modest fortune operating barbershops in Natchez, Mississippi, in the 1830s and 1840s. He kept detailed records of his business and personal life.

In Philadelphia, hairdresser Joseph Cassey made wigs and lent money. Sailmaker, abolitionist, and inventor James Forten (1766–1842) made a fortune in the maritime industry, in which blacks were represented at every level. Former slave Stephen Smith and black abolitionist William Whipper were partners in a successful lumber business in Pennsylvania.

New Orleans merchant Cecee McCarty owned thirty-two slaves, which she used to help sell imported dry goods throughout Louisiana. She accumulated a fortune of $155,000.

According to New York City tax records before 1855, there were twenty-one black businessmen who made more than $100,000 a year.

owner's will. Some had escaped to freedom. More than half of these free blacks lived in the South. Still, if a person had dark skin, it was up to him or her to prove that he or she was not a slave.

Did any free blacks own slaves?

Some free blacks did own slaves. Others bought their own relatives to get them out of slavery. There were also a number of skilled free blacks, such as tailors, shoemakers, and carpenters, who bought slaves and made them apprentices. In 1850, 19 percent of the black tailors in Charleston, South Carolina, owned slaves. According to the 1830 census, 753 blacks in New Orleans, Louisiana, owned slaves. Slaves were also used by free blacks as maids or day workers. A small number of blacks owned slaves for the same reason as whites did: to perform the labor in their moneymaking operations, such as farms.

Did any free blacks own businesses?

Although most blacks were held in slavery in the 1700s and 1800s, and despite the fact that economic opportuni-

Early Black Churches in America

The first known black church in America, the African Baptist or Bluestone Church, was established in 1758 on the William Byrd plantation in Mecklenberg, Virginia. The church was named after the nearby Bluestone River.

Around 1774, the Silver Bluff Baptist Church in Silver Bluff, South Carolina, was founded by a slave preacher named George Liele. About 1788, a slave baptized by Liele founded the First African Baptist Church in Savannah, Georgia. By 1800, more than 25,000 African Americans were attending other independent black Baptist churches that had been formed in North Carolina, South Carolina, and Virginia.

In 1816, African Americans in Philadelphia, led by Richard Allen, founded what became the African Methodist Episcopal Church. In 1821, blacks in New York City formed the African Methodist Episcopal Zion Church.

ties were rare and risky, even for free blacks, a few free blacks owned businesses. Some, mostly in the North, owned construction companies, inns, tailor shops, or other businesses.

Did free black people lead a normal life?

For free blacks, being free did not mean living freely. State laws in every region restricted the rights of free blacks, often limiting their ability to earn a living. In Maryland and North Carolina, for instance, free blacks had to have special licenses to sell corn, wheat, or tobacco. At all times, free blacks had to carry a certificate of freedom. If they were caught without it, they risked being kidnapped and sold into slavery by dishonest slave traders.

Whether in the North or South, free blacks did not have all the rights of citizens. They were not permitted to vote or to hold public office. They were also not allowed to testify in court against whites, and they could not carry weapons. If they failed to pay their debts or taxes, they were at risk of being enslaved as a penalty.

How did slaves adapt to American culture?

Although white slaveholders tried to suppress African culture (they believed slaves could be controlled more easily if they spoke only English and depended on what the slaveholders taught them), slaves created their own African American culture by combining English and Christianity with their African culture. They recognized their African

script, Banneker included a letter in which he protested slavery and disputed Jefferson's claim that blacks were intellectually inferior to whites. Abolitionists used the almanacs as evidence of the intellectual capabilities of blacks. In 1789, President George Washington had appointed Banneker to the commission planning the construction of Washington, D.C. Banneker helped survey the future site of the national capital between 1790 and 1793.

Did slaves ever sue for their freedom?

Many slaves did sue for their freedom, but these freedom suits did not challenge slavery itself. They alleged that the slave was being unlawfully held in bondage. In one 1735 case, *Re Negro James,* a slave named James petitioned a Massachusetts court for his future freedom, since his master's will stated that James would be freed when the master's wife died. The master's son, who felt he owned James, fought the petition. But in 1737, after his mistress died, James was finally declared free.

In 1846, a Virginia-born slave named Dred Scott sued for his and his family's freedom, on the grounds that they lived on free soil (his master had moved into a free state). His case, *Scott v. Sanford,* eventually went to the U.S. Supreme Court. But in 1857, the Court ruled against Scott. The ruling stated that slaves owned on free soil were still slaves, and added that Scott, because he was black, was not qualified to sue. Chief Justice Roger B. Taney wrote, in his opinion, that black women and men were an "inferior class of beings" who "had no rights which the white man was bound to respect."

Did slaves ever use violence to protest slavery?

There were many instances of violent slave revolts. These were very desperate actions, because they were doomed to fail. The most famous slave revolts were led by Gabriel Prosser, Nat Turner, and Denmark Vesey.

The first major slave uprising in America happened in 1739. In the early morning hours of September 9, approximately twenty slaves gathered at the Stono River near Charleston, South Carolina. After killing two storekeepers,

Slaves Revolt

In 1800, inspired partly by the biblical story of Moses leading the Israelites out of bondage, Virginia slave Gabriel Prosser planned to attack and seize parts of the city of Richmond, killing as many whites as possible in the process. He spread word of his plan to over one thousand slaves; they gathered, only to break up during a rainstorm. Three slaves had told their masters of the plot, and troops captured at least three dozen plotters. Prosser hid for a month, but finally was captured. All were tried and hanged.

1822: Denmark Vesey, a carpenter who had bought his freedom in 1800 with money from a winning lottery ticket, hated slavery and made speeches and sermons against it. In Charleston, South Carolina, more than 9,000 slaves and free blacks were attracted to Vesey's plot to "liberate" the city. Several slaves betrayed the plot, and Vesey and some of his comrades were arrested and hanged.

1831: Nat Turner, a Virginia slave and preacher, planned the most famous slave revolt in American history. He began with just six slaves, who went to the plantation of Turner's master on August 22 and killed the entire family. By the next morning, the group, now numbering sixty, had traveled through the county, killing at least fifty-seven white men, women, and children. Police and the military captured or killed many of the rebels, but Turner escaped arrest until October 30, when he was captured and hanged.

they marched along the main road, burning plantations and shooting and killing more than twenty whites. They marched for over ten miles without being stopped. But later that afternoon, the group, which had grown to one hundred slaves, was surrounded by armed whites who shot the slaves and cut off their heads, which they put up on spikes along the road as a warning to other slaves.

The largest slave rebellion in U.S. history was the Louisiana uprising of 1811. It involved over 300 slaves near New Orleans. Beginning at the plantation of a slave owner called Major Andre, the slaves marched toward the city, burning plantations and killing two or three whites. Soldiers killed sixty-six of them immediately, and sixteen other leaders were later tried and executed. Again, their heads were cut off and placed on spikes along the road.

In 1831, Nat Turner led sixty slaves in the most famous slave revolt in American history, which left at least fifty-seven people dead. The revolt had a tremendous impact on the South and led to harsh restrictions.

The white abolitionist John Brown (1800–1859) was very much against slavery, like his father had been. His opinion was that slavery could only be ended by force. On October 16, 1859, Brown and eighteen men, including several of his sons and five blacks, seized control of the U.S. Arsenal at Harpers Ferry, Virginia (now West Virginia), as well as the town. After the group was surrounded by the local militia, ten of Brown's men, including two of his sons, were killed; Brown was wounded and forced to surrender. Arrested and charged with various crimes, including treason and murder, Brown was convicted and hanged.

After each rebellion, slave codes were made stronger and punishments became more severe.

Did any slaves ever try to escape?

According to census reports for the years 1855 to 1865, one thousand slaves fled each year; however, that number was a small fraction of the total. Slaves in the deep South usually did not run away to the North because it was too far. Instead, they hid in the wilderness. There, groups of runaways that became known as maroon communities were formed. The North was easier to reach for slaves who fled from Delaware, Kentucky, Maryland, Missouri, Tennessee, and Virginia. Many were helped by the **Underground Railroad.**

What was the Underground Railroad?

The Underground Railroad was the name given to a secret network of houses and people who illegally helped escaping slaves reach safety in the non-slave states or Canada in the period before the American Civil War. It was also called the Liberty Line. The name also referred to the escape routes through the North as well as some that led south to other countries. Many people who believed that slavery was wrong offered their homes, churches, and services to the Underground Railroad.

Each safe place along the Underground Railroad was called a station. Escaping slaves were called passengers, and those who helped them were called conductors.

The Underground Railroad began in the 1780s under the Quakers. Northern free blacks played an important role in planning, communication, and decision making within the network. The Underground Railroad was most active in Pennsylvania, Indiana, and Ohio, and existed in most states in the North. It is estimated that between 50,000 and 100,000 escaped slaves were aided by the Underground Railroad.

What were the escaping slaves' destinations?

When possible, conductors met them at Cincinnati, Ohio, and Wilmington, Delaware, which were at the northern borders of the slave states. Those escaping to Canada went to the lake ports of Detroit, Michigan; Sandusky, Ohio; Erie, Pennsylvania; and Buffalo, New York, where they could sail north.

How did the Underground Railroad help slaves escape?

Most of the fugitives came from the states of the upper South—such as Maryland, Virginia, and Kentucky—because these states were closest to the North. They were

claimed by anyone who found it, and the two Americans claimed it.

The owners of the ship demanded that the ship and the slaves be turned over to them. Meanwhile, local abolitionists joined together to help the Africans. In a case that was eventually appealed all the way to the Supreme Court, the Africans were declared free. They returned to Africa in 1842.

Who else tried to help the slaves?

In 1833, the American Anti-Slavery Society was established in Philadelphia to advance the abolition of slavery in the United States. The first such society in America, it was made up of smaller local groups. The American Anti-Slavery Society was formed by Theodore Dwight Weld (1803–1895), Arthur Tappan (1786–1865), and Lewis Tappan (1788–1873), who were militant in the fight against slavery. The society operated until 1870, when the adoption of the Fifteenth Amendment to the U.S. Constitution granted citizenship to blacks.

What did abolitionists do to fight slavery?

Abolitionists had many methods and ideas. The Reverend Henry Highland Garnet called for a slave uprising at an 1843 meeting of black representatives. Harriet Tubman, Sojourner Truth, Maria Stewart, and others helped slaves escape through the Underground Railroad.

Songs of Protest

Slave songs, also called spirituals, were songs of sorrow and hope, created by the slaves. They contained words or messages about their longing for freedom or their coming reward in heaven for their suffering on earth, as this example demonstrates:

> *Nobody knows de trouble I see*
> *Nobody knows but Jesus*
> *Nobody knows de trouble I see*
> *Glory, Hallelujah!*
> *Sometimes I'm up, sometimes I'm*
> *   down, Oh yes Lord*
> *Sometimes I'm almos' to de groun,*
> *   Oh yes Lord*
> *Although you see me goin' 'long*
> *   so, Oh yes Lord*
> *I have my trials here below,*
> *   Oh yes Lord.*

Some spirituals were a means of communication. Slaves used lyrics to notify one another of a secret gathering:

> *I take my text in Matthew, and by*
> *   Revelation,*
> *I know you by your garment.*
> *Dere's a meeting here tonight,*
> *Dere's a meeting here tonight.*

Songs were also used to warn workers of an approaching master or overseer coming to check on them:

> *Sister, carry de news on,*
> *Master's in de field;*
> *Sister, carry de news on,*
> *Master's in de field.*

Some fought slavery with the pen. Theodore Dwight Weld collected stories from slaves, slave owners, and slave traders. His 200-page book, *American Slavery As It Is: Testimony of a Thousand Witnesses*, describing the horrors of slavery, was published in 1839, selling more than 100,000 copies.

In 1847, Frederick Douglass joined with Martin Delany (1812–1855), a doctor, essayist, and black nationalist, to establish the *North Star*, an independent black journal. In 1851, Harriet Beecher Stowe wrote a book called *Uncle Tom's Cabin*. Based on true stories, it told about the hard life of some slaves in Kentucky. Millions of people read Stowe's book, and it had a tremendous impact on public opinion.

What other tools were used in the struggle for freedom?

By the early 1800s, writing had became an important part of the black struggle for freedom. It gave blacks a way to defend themselves publicly and share information quickly. In 1793, Thomas Gray, Absalom Jones, and Richard Allen (1760–1831), three prominent black leaders in Philadelphia, published long essays denouncing those who supported slavery and treated free blacks unfairly. These writings were distributed at black churches, antislavery meetings, and other gatherings in the free North.

On March 16, 1827, John B. Russwurm and Samuel E. Cornish published the first black newspaper, *Freedom's Journal*, to answer a series of attacks on the black community that had been made in a white New York newspaper. It was published for over three years. By the Civil War (1861–1865), over forty publications were being issued by blacks.

What were some of the social networks free blacks had in the late 1700s and early 1800s?

In Boston, Massachusetts; Philadelphia, Pennsylvania; and Providence, Rhode Island, antislavery crusader Prince Hall (1735–1807) organized a group of Masonic lodges for blacks beginning with African Lodge #459, America's first black fraternal organization. By 1831, black communities in many cities had churches, fraternal orders, schools, and political organizations. Most of them were established to

Women Abolitionists

One of the most memorable abolitionists of her time, the dark, tall, and plainly dressed woman calling herself Sojourner Truth was born into slavery in 1797. After enduring years of physical and emotional abuse, Truth was freed in 1827 under New York State law. The bold, independent-minded Truth went on to become a moving and powerful preacher, speaking at national meetings and conventions about black and women's rights. She is perhaps best known for her speech in which she stridently defended women's political importance declaring, "I have plowed and planted and gathered into barns, and no man could head me—and ar'n't I a woman?"

Another unlikely heroine who played a great role in the fight against slavery was the white writer Harriet Beecher Stowe (1811–1896). Enraged at the Fugitive Slave Law, Stowe wrote the most popular piece of literature of the nineteenth century, *Uncle Tom's Cabin*. This melodramatic, sentimental novel became one of the all-time best-selling books in American history, and its sympathetic portrayal of slave life infuriated the South so much that they publicly burned copies of the novel and arrested anyone who owned one. *Uncle Tom's Cabin* helped millions of Americans understand the horrors of slavery.

help blacks become educated and informed. Many provided financial help for members' families that suffered illness or death. Forming these organizations took courage, because in many states it was illegal for African Americans to gather together.

They also had their own publications including newspapers, such as *Freedom's Journal* founded in 1827, and militant pamphlets, including *Appeal* (1829), by David Walker. These publications spread the words and thoughts of blacks on their condition and desires. During the 1830s, black leaders held national conventions every year to discuss strategies for racial advancement.

How were free blacks treated in America in the 1800s?

Discrimination against free blacks was very strong throughout the United States. Although African Americans could vote in some northern states in the years after the

Black Artisans and Inventors

Slaves played significant parts in the design and construction of plantations, churches, mansions, and public buildings. John Hemings was a slave artisan who managed the woodwork, or joiner's, shop at Monticello, President Thomas Jefferson's Virginia plantation. Hemings created at least eight items of furniture designed by Jefferson, bringing the president's sketches to life as chairs, tables, and benches. Hemings also created fine woodwork such as railings, arches, and window shutters. His work can be seen today at Monticello, and reproductions of some of his work are for sale.

Slaves could not be granted patents for any inventions that they created until after the Civil War. As a result, the efforts of slaves were ignored or, if accepted, credited to their masters.

The first black to be granted a patent is believed to have been Henry Blair. In 1834, he received a patent for a seed planter.

Norbert Rillieux (1806–1894), educated in France, was the son of a slave mother and a wealthy white engineer. In 1846, he received a patent for a vacuum evaporator that turned sugarcane juice into white sugar crystals. The invention revolutionized the sugar industry and was adapted for use in the manufacturing of soap, gelatin, glue, and other products.

Lewis Temple (1800–1854) lived in New Bedford, Massachusetts, where he made harpoons for New England whalers. He invented a new kind of harpoon that was called the most important invention in the history of whaling. He did not have a patent for his revolutionary new harpoon and died penniless.

George Washington Carver (1864–1943), born a slave, obtained his degree in agricultural science while working as the college janitor. He devoted his life to researching agricultural products. He is famous for deriving more than 300 products from the peanut and 118 from the sweet potato. He convinced southern farmers to plant peanuts, sweet potatoes, and other crops instead of cotton, which was depleting the soil. He never patented his discoveries.

By 1913, an estimated one thousand patents were issued to blacks for their inventions. Black patent holders included

Jan Matzeliger: shoe last
Elijah McCoy: machine
    lubricating machine
C. B. Brooks: street sweeper
G. F. Grant: golf tee
William Purvis: paper bag
    making machine
G. T. Sampson: clothes dryer
J. R. Winters: fire escape ladder

Revolutionary War, there were laws limiting black political participation, ownership of land, and social contact with whites. In 1829 a white mob attacked an African American community in Cincinnati. During the next few years, similar riots took place in other northern cities where white workers resented black competition for jobs. By the 1830s, most Southern and some northern states restricted or prohibited the entry of free blacks. African Americans were barred from public education facilities, good housing, and legal protection in many cities.

Did any American blacks want to return to Africa?

In the early 1800s, abolitionists, free blacks, politicians, religious leaders, and even President Thomas Jefferson debated whether sending blacks back to Africa would solve the problem of slavery. The idea was called the **Return to Africa** movement. Not everyone agreed. The abolitionist David Walker said, "America is more our country than it is the whites'. We have enriched it with our blood and tears." Antislavery leader Frederick Douglass felt the same way.

Two free blacks who were in favor of the idea were Paul Cuffe and Edward Wilmont Blyden. They felt blacks could only be truly free living in their homeland. In 1815, Cuffe took thirty-eight free blacks to Sierra Leone, in West Africa, to settle them there.

In 1816, a group of white abolitionists formed the **American Colonization Society** (ACS), a private corporation to help blacks return to Africa. Many prominent whites gave large donations.

In the 1850s, antislavery minister Reverend Henry Highland Garnet and black nationalist Martin Delany decided that blacks could progress only by remaining separate from whites. In 1859, Delany led an expedition to Africa to investigate the possibilities of setting up colonies. He later published an official report with recommendations for returning blacks to Africa.

Did any blacks actually return to Africa?

On April 25, 1822, a group of black settlers, sponsored by the ACS, landed at Cape Mesurado in Liberia. By 1839, they had formed a commonwealth and had elected a governor, Thomas Buchanan (a black cousin of James Buchanan, the fifteenth president of the United States). In 1847, the area known as Liberia became an independent republic. Nearly 3,000 blacks had emigrated there.

However, most of them found it difficult to adjust to a new country because they were used to America. Even though their roots were in Africa, they brought many American beliefs and values with them. Some even felt they were better than the people who already lived in Liberia, which caused resentment and hostility. The ACS was never able to get large numbers of blacks to emigrate to Liberia, partly because many blacks felt that they should not abandon their enslaved brothers and sisters.

What state first ended slavery?

After 1773, the northern states slowly eliminated slavery because their industries did not need to use slave labor. In 1777, Vermont became the first state to abolish slavery outright.

How did slavery end?

In 1860, the slave-owning southern states began to worry that they would lose their power, perhaps even their slaves, under newly elected President Abraham Lincoln, a Republican. Between November 1860 and February 1861, those states **seceded,** or broke away, from the United States, renamed themselves the Confederate States of America (they were also known as the **Confederacy,** or the rebel states), and elected their own president. The Civil War broke out in April 1861 between the Confederate states and the Northern states, known as the **Union.**

The commanders of the Union army disobeyed President Lincoln's order to return runaway slaves to the Confederacy. They set them free and let them join the Union army. This, along with the need for more soldiers, may have forced Lincoln to issue the Emancipation Proclamation in 1863, which freed all slaves in areas controlled by the Confederacy.

Early Black Publications (1827–1860)

Freedom's Journal (New York City, 1827–1829)

Rights of All (New York City, 1829)

Weekly Advocate (New York City, 1837)

Colored American (New York City, 1837–1841)

National Reformer (Philadelphia, Pennsylvania, 1838–1839)

Mirror of Liberty (New York City, 1838–1840)

Northern Star and Freemen's Advocate (Albany, New York, 1842)

Mystery (Pittsburgh, Pennsylvania, 1843–1847)

Ram's Horn (New York City, 1846–1848)

North Star (Rochester, New York, 1847–1851)

Aliened American (Cleveland, Ohio, 1852–1856)

Christian Recorder (Philadelphia, Pennsylvania, 1852–1860)

Mirror of the Times (San Francisco, California, 1855)

Frederick Douglass's Paper (Rochester, New York, 1851–1859)

Douglass's Monthly (Rochester, New York, 1859–1860)

Weekly Anglo-African (New York City, 1859–1860)

Anglo-African Magazine (New York City, 1859–1861)

The Union victory in the Civil War brought freedom to nearly 4 million blacks. But the attitudes that had sustained slavery in the South for more than 300 years did not end with the war.

What was the Civil War?

The Civil War (also known as the War Between the States and the War of Southern Independence) was a military conflict between the United States of America (the Union) and eleven secessionist Southern states, organized as the Confederate States of America (the Confederacy). It took place between the years 1861 and 1865, and was won by the Union.

What caused the Civil War?

For forty years, the North and South had been resentful of each other for economic, social, and political reasons. The South was agricultural and produced crops such as cotton, tobacco, and sugarcane for export to the North or to Europe. But it depended on the North for manufacturing

At one point during the Civil War, black soldiers in the U.S. Colored Troops were paid only $7 a month for their service.

and business services important for trading. In addition, the South had almost 4 million slaves—which was the largest single investment in the South. Although the number of slave owners was small, they ruled Southern politics and society. Southerners who did not have slaves were still loyal to the system because they were afraid of slave revolts.

The 54th Massachusetts Colored Infantry, led by Sergeant William H. Carney, showed valor and heroism when they attacked Fort Wayne in South Carolina, 1863.

Did blacks fight in the Civil War?

After President Lincoln issued his Emancipation Proclamation, blacks rushed to join up to help the North win the war. A total of 178,985 fought in the war; 37,000 were killed in action and seventeen black soldiers and sailors were awarded the Congressional Medal of Honor, the highest award for bravery in the United States.

The South refused to enlist blacks into the Confederate army until March 1865. Recognizing that the South was los-

Did black women fight in the Civil War?

Harriet Tubman left her husband and brothers behind when she escaped from slavery, and her intelligence had enabled her to free hundreds of slaves without getting caught. She used this same ability in the Union army, where she served as a spy and a nurse during the Civil War. Her bravery and mastery of the rifle gained her the respect of the men who fought with her. To them she became affectionately known as "General" Harriet Tubman.

Susie King Taylor (1842–1912), also an escaped slave, ran away at the age of twelve. By the time she was sixteen, she was teaching freed blacks to read and write. After meeting Clara Barton, founder of the American Red Cross, Susie wanted to help black Civil War troops. She traveled with the 33rd U.S. Colored Troops as a nurse and launderer until the end of the Civil War.

When did slavery officially end?

In 1865, the Thirteenth Amendment to the Constitution was passed, abolishing slavery in the entire United States.

What changed for slaves after Emancipation?
What protections did the freed slaves have? ◆ W
did the slaves ...... ◆ ...... at w
sharecropping? ◆ What was the period
Reconstruction? ◆ What other assistance was gi
o freed slaves? ◆ ...... the Freedmen's Bur
do to help the freed slaves? ◆ What else did
gov..ment do to help blacks during Reconstruction
◆ ...... America .... a .... ..age
their new freedom? ◆ Did blacks participate
politics during Reconstruction? ◆ Were any Afric

EMANCIPATION AND RECONSTRUCTION

What changed for slaves after Emancipation?

After more than 200 years of slavery, African Americans now saw a chance to work for themselves by farming their own land and using their skills to make a living. It was now legal for them to come and go whenever they wanted, to learn to read and write, to stay with their families, and to be married. Most importantly, they could no longer be bought and sold.

What protections did the freed slaves have?

President Lincoln pushed for strong laws to help the 4 million former slaves. Congress passed, and the states ratified, the Thirteenth, Fourteenth, and Fifteenth Amendments to the Constitution.

The Thirteenth Amendment, passed in 1865, stated that enslavement of any group of people was forever unlawful. The Fourteenth Amendment, passed in 1866, stated that every person born in the United States was a citizen of the United States and the state in which they reside. The Fifteenth Amendment, passed in 1870, stated that the right to vote shall not be denied because of race or the fact that a person was a former slave.

Remember, only men were allowed to vote in the United States when these amendments were passed; women were not allowed to vote.

What did the slaves do after Emancipation?

Many tested their freedom by leaving their slave owners to go in search of lost relatives. Some adventurers took off with no special destination in mind. But few of the freed slaves (or freedmen, as they were called) had the experience or skills to begin an independent life. Most could not read or write, and did not even know how to use money. In many cases, **sharecropping** replaced slavery.

What was sharecropping?

In sharecropping, poor blacks and whites sold their labor to planters for a share of the crop. The planter sold them cabins, work animals, tools, food, clothes, and other supplies on credit. At the end of the season, the sharecropper would pay off his debts with profits from the crop. But planters charged whatever they liked, then added interest, which caused the sharecroppers to get deeper into debt each season. Their wages kept them alive, but very few could do anything to better their impoverished conditions.

What was the period of Reconstruction?

Between 1865 and 1877 the U.S. government passed laws that helped protect the rights of all free people in the United States. This period was called **Reconstruction,** because it was supposed to lead to a reconstructed, or repaired, society that included people of all races.

How did the freed slaves prepare themselves to be a part of American life after slavery ended?

After the end of the Civil War, blacks all over the United States gathered in groups of all sizes to discuss their future in America and American politics. One such gathering was the Colored National Convention, held April 5 to 7, 1876, in Nashville, Tennessee. There they discussed social and political issues such as who they should vote for, what laws they should get changed, and what new laws they should suggest.

In 1879 more Colored Conventions were held in New Orleans, Vicksburg, and Nashville. The Nashville group recommended that a request be made to the national government that $500,000 be appropriated "to aid in the removal of our people from the South."

What other assistance was given to freed slaves?

The Bureau of Refugees, Freedmen, and Abandoned Lands (or the **Freedmen's Bureau,** as it was called), was created by the U.S. War Department to provide basic health and educational services to help make the slaves' changeover to freedom easier. It existed from 1865 to 1872. There were about one hundred other privately financed freedmen's aid societies ready to lend a helping hand.

What did the Freedmen's Bureau do to help the freed slaves?

The Freedmen's Bureau, run by Major General Oliver O. Howard, offered a variety of services. It distributed food and clothing to freedmen who had been made homeless by the Civil War, and rented to them up to forty acres of land that had been abandoned or confiscated. Its health program established forty hospitals, and treated nearly half a million cases of illness. The bureau also established more than 4,000 schools, from the elementary grades through college. It charged no tuition and often provided free textbooks. Almost 250,000 former slaves received varying amounts of education through the schools established by the Freedmen's Bureau.

The bureau also acted as legal guardian to the freedmen, and ruled on cases in its own courts. To protect the former slaves in their negotiations with landowners, the bureau prepared labor contracts calling for a fair wage. The Freedmen's Bureau had the power to enforce these contracts.

In 1872, Congress decided not to renew the Freedmen's Bureau, and it ceased to exist.

The Freedmen's Savings and Trust Company, a bank, was successful at first. By 1872, more than 70,000 African American deposi-

More Than School

Black schools were tremendously important to the African American community in the late nineteenth century. In addition to providing education, these schools also trained farmers and published newspapers. They educated blacks about land acquisition and encouraged more active participation in politics and government as well.

Southern whites became incensed about the existence of these schools and resented the new opportunities offered to African Americans. School burning was one of the most visible ways whites showed their anger.

In 1867, Major General Oliver O. Howard founded Howard University, located in Washington, D.C. The university was named for him, and he served as its third president.

The Civil Rights Act of 1875 was the last legislation enacted during Reconstruction.

tors had placed a total of $3.7 million in the bank's thirty-four branches. Two years later, deposits reached $55 million. But the bank, although organized by the federal government, did not have the government's backing. In 1874 it collapsed, a victim of the financial panic of 1873, inexperienced management, and a number of irregular loans to white businessmen. Its depositors were left penniless.

What else did the government do to help blacks during Reconstruction?

On March 13, 1866, Congress passed an act, called the Civil Rights Act of 1866, which stated that all persons born in the United States were citizens with full rights and privileges of citizenship under the Constitution.

In 1875, a second civil rights act, called the Civil Rights Act of 1875, was enacted. It stated that all persons, even former slaves, were entitled to use public accommodations; that all persons, regardless of race, were allowed to serve on juries; and that anyone denying a person these civil rights could be punished.

How did African Americans take advantage of their new freedom?

When the Fifteenth Amendment was passed, the large numbers of new black voters meant that blacks were finally participating in government. The Freedmen's Bureau helped African Americans build schools, small businesses, and churches. Several black colleges were founded during this time. White teachers came to the South, opened schools, and trained other teachers; ministers and businessmen helped with voter registration.

Young black men became interested in political office. Many African Americans were elected to positions of power on the local,

Higher Education

In 1862, the Morril Act was created to provide funding for land grants for higher education. In 1890, the second Morril Act (or Land Grant Act) was passed. This act stated that the government had to pay for the creation and maintenance of technical and agricultural schools for blacks if they were going to provide funding for technical and agricultural schools for whites.

This land grant system paved the way for black higher education in the South.

Black Colleges Founded During Reconstruction

Knoxville College, Tennessee (1863)

Fisk University, Tennessee (1866)

Emerson College, Alabama (1867)

Howard University, Washington, D.C. (1867); Howard University Medical School (1868); and Howard University Law School (1871)

Morehouse College, Georgia (1867)

Morgan State College, Baltimore, Maryland (1867)

Johnson C. Smith College, North Carolina (1867)

Talladega College, Alabama (1867)

Hampton University, Virginia (1868)

Dillard University, New Orleans, Louisiana (1869)

Tougaloo College, Mississippi (1869)

LeMoyne-Owen College, Memphis, Tennessee (1870)

state, and national levels. African Americans in political office used their power to improve public education and to end property qualifications for voting, imprisonment for debt, and segregation in public facilities. In South Carolina, blacks held the most political positions, holding at various times the offices of lieutenant governor, secretary of state, treasurer, and speaker of the house.

Did blacks participate in politics during Reconstruction?

Some free northern blacks were already participating in politics. Many worked with white elected officials to abolish slavery. What they learned enabled them to help other African Americans understand how the U.S. government operated. Many of these northern blacks moved to the South after the Civil War, so that they could work where the majority of the population was black. Because President Lincoln, who had freed the slaves, was a Republican, most African Americans were major supporters of the Republican Party.

In 1870, Richard Greener became the first black to graduate from Harvard University; he later became dean of Howard Law School in 1879.

Were any African Americans elected to political office during Reconstruction?

Because Alabama, Mississippi, South Carolina, and Georgia had the largest African American populations,

During Reconstruction, fourteen African Americans were elected to the House of Representatives and two served in the Senate.

In 1872, Charlotte Ray received her law degree from Howard University Law School, making her the first black woman lawyer.

those states had some of the first black elected politicians beginning in 1867. John Willis Menard of Louisiana and Jefferson F. Long of Georgia were among the first African Americans elected to Congress (in 1868 and 1870, respectively). In Louisiana, the black lieutenant governor P. B. S. Pinchback served as acting governor for some time after the white governor was removed from office in 1872. He was later elected to the U.S. Senate. Two black men—Hiram R. Revels and Blanche K. Bruce—became U.S. senators, and some fourteen African Americans served in the House of Representatives. Thirteen of the fourteen blacks who served in Congress during Reconstruction were ex-slaves, but all were well educated, either self-taught or formally trained. There were seven lawyers, three ministers, one banker, one publisher, two school teachers, and three college presidents among them.

What was life like for black politicians during Reconstruction?

Life was hard for the black politicians. They were sel-

Blacks in Congress During Reconstruction (1865–1875)

Hiram R. Revels (Mississippi), 1870–1871: The first black U.S. senator; in 1852, as pastor at the St. Paul AME Church in St. Louis, he defied the law by allowing slaves to worship in his church and starting a school to teach black children to read and write.

Blanche K. Bruce (Mississippi), 1875–1881: A former slave, he was educated at Oberlin College and was a tax assessor and sheriff before becoming the first black man to serve a full six-year term in the U.S. Senate.

Robert Smalls (South Carolina), 1875–1879 and 1881–1887: Born a slave, he fought in the Confederate army as a seaman, and was commended for his heroic act of delivering his ship to the Union army. After his term in Congress, President Benjamin Harrison appointed him collector of the port of Beaufort, South Carolina, his birthplace.

Joseph H. Rainey (South Carolina), 1870–1879

Jefferson F. Long (Georgia), 1870–1871

Benjamin S. Turner (Alabama), 1871–1873

Robert C. DeLarge (South Carolina), 1871–1873

Robert B. Elliott (South Carolina), 1871–1875

Josiah T. Walls (Florida), 1871–1877

Richard H. Cain (South Carolina), 1873–1875 and 1877–1879

Alonzo J. Ransier (South Carolina), 1873–1875

James T. Rapier (Alabama), 1873–1875

John R. Lynch (Mississippi), 1873–1877, 1882–1883

Jeremiah Haralson (Alabama), 1875–1877

John A. Hyman (North Carolina), 1875–1877

Charles E. Nash (Louisiana), 1875–1877

dom appointed to important committee chairmanships. They were not invited to socialize and did not receive special benefits that other congressmen did. They could not get into restaurants or hotels in the downtown Washington, D.C. area, and had to sleep at the homes of friends or the colored Young Men's Christian Association (YMCA). They had to bring their lunches, go to restaurants in black neighborhoods, or eat in the basement of the Capitol with other black employees. Despite their intelligence, they were often called illiterate, ignorant, and incompetent.

How did the presence of African Americans change the political system?

As more blacks participated in politics, the black vote became important. African Americans filled many elected and appointed positions, including those of sheriff, mayor, prosecuting attorney, justice of the peace, and county superintendent of education. Mississippi, Louisiana, and South Carolina each elected black lieutenant governors.

Many changes were made in federal, state, and local laws. For example, laws allowing whipping and branding as punishment were abolished throughout the South. Imprisonment for debt was abolished in many states. Several states adopted new constitutions that removed property qualifications and tests for voting and holding office. Each constitution provided for a statewide system of free public education.

Did the new amendments and laws passed during Reconstruction erase racism?

Most white Southerners—even if they had been too poor to have been slave owners—refused to accept freedmen as citizens who had rights equal to their own. Many whites were extremely angry, and white hate groups such as the **Ku Klux Klan (KKK)** began to harass and physically attack African Americans who tried to exercise their new rights. Black schools, churches, and homes were burned. Whites who supported black voting rights were given the same treatment. Southern states put together governments that deliberately excluded African American citizens from the democratic process, and state legislatures enacted **Black Codes,** which prevented African Americans from using their new rights. Southern leaders argued that the government had acted out of order by giving former slaves equal rights and protection under the law. **White supremacy** became the motto, and **states' rights** became the method used to pass and uphold the racist Black Codes.

What kind of laws were included in the Black Codes?

These black codes, enacted to control former slaves in the South, were much stricter in some states than in others.

In certain states, blacks could testify in court, but only in cases involving other blacks. South Carolina forbade freed blacks without a special license from doing any work except farming and menial jobs. Additionally, African Americans could not leave their jobs without giving up any back pay they were owed, which was often substantial.

"Masters" were allowed to whip "servants" under 18 years of age. In other states, African Americans could be punished for making what were deemed insulting gestures and seditious speeches.

What are states' rights?

Under the Constitution, power is divided between the national (also known as federal) government and the state governments. The national government has the power to enforce constitutional laws. Each state has the power to regulate matters inside the state as long as they are within constitutional law. These powers are sometimes called states' rights.

Those who were in favor of states' rights protested that the government was overstepping its bounds by acting on behalf of former slaves in the areas of education, employment, voting rights, and other matters the states felt they controlled.

How did whites react to black progress?

Many southern whites were still bitter about the abolition of slavery, and they feared the power that African Americans could have in the government. They did all they could to keep blacks from participating in government, including threatening voters, destroying homes, and even injuring or killing black elected officials. During the 1890s, more than one thousand African Americans were killed in the United States by widespread **lynching** (or mob killing of a per-

Mob Rule

In April 1873, a mob of whites murdered 105 African American citizens in Colfax, Louisiana, following a dispute over election results. Although three were convicted of violating the blacks' civil rights, the convictions were later overturned by the U.S. Supreme Court, which ruled that the mob constituted a private army, and that the federal government therefore had no authority over the matter.

son, especially by hanging). Soon, white majorities regained control of state governments, which passed stronger laws that denied blacks access to the political process.

In 1877, states began to pass laws permitting **segregation** (the separation of a group of people according to their race): South Carolina made it a crime for black and white cotton mill workers to look out the same window. Florida required "Negro" textbooks and "white" textbooks. Oklahoma required separate but equal telephone booths. In 1883, the Civil Rights Act of 1875 was declared unconstitutional by the Supreme Court.

In 1896, in the *Plessy v. Ferguson* case, the U.S. Supreme Court ruled that separate but equal facilities (that is, the same accommodations for blacks as for whites, only separate) were legal. This set the stage for legal segregation and discrimination, the practice of treating people differently because of their skin color. By the end of the century, the Fifteenth Amendment's guarantees of voting rights for African Americans had been virtually erased through tactics such as **poll taxes** and **literacy tests.**

What were poll taxes?

Poll taxes were taxes that only blacks were required to pay if they wanted to vote. The rules on paying these taxes

Segregation and Jim Crow

After Reconstruction, southern states enacted laws that made it nearly impossible for blacks to vote, which meant that political power was now held solely by whites. Where the races had been previously separated by habit, they were now separated by law. These laws were also called Jim Crow laws.

Jim Crow was a buffoonish minstrel show character created in 1828 by a white entertainer named Thomas D. Rice, and was based on an elderly black slave who danced and sang as he worked. The segregationist laws were named Jim Crow laws because the character was used to stereotype African Americans.

This legalized segregation included hotels, restaurants, toilets, sidewalks, libraries, schools, drinking fountains, parks, playgrounds, hospitals, prisons, and transportation.

were deliberately confusing and unfair. Poll taxes were used throughout the South as a way to stop African Americans from voting.

What were literacy tests?

Whenever blacks came to register to vote, some southern states, such as Mississippi and South Carolina, required registrants who could not read to interpret a section of the state's constitution after it was read aloud to them. Another test, the good-character test, required a registrant to bring a responsible witness along to vouch for his worth and standing. In other tests, questions such as "How many bubbles are in a bar of soap?" were asked. Registrants who failed were not allowed to vote.

No such tests were given to white registrants.

What were lynchings?

Lynchings were murders committed by mobs of whites; the victims were usually black. The most common reasons they were killed were that they were too outspoken against racism, or too successful. Many African Americans were lynched during and after Reconstruction, and whites who were sympathetic to black causes were also victims. *Crisis* magazine, published by the National Association for the Advancement of Colored People (NAACP), regularly ran photos of lynching victims so that the country could see the effects of racism. The last recorded lynching in the United States took place in 1964. The victim of that attack was the 4,743rd person known to die in a lynching in the United States since 1882.

What happened to whites who lynched blacks?

Lynching was considered a form of law enforcement; after all, whippings of African Americans had been legal and common ever since slavery had begun. Lynchings were often covered by the local white press as if they were normal events, and white people very rarely (if ever at all) went to jail for injuring or killing a black person. On the other hand, any African American with the nerve to complain to the authorities of physical violence would see his assailant go free, and would himself probably be sent to jail or the chain gang.

Originally formed in 1866 as a social club, by 1868 the Ku Klux Klan had become a violent terrorist organization dedicated to forcing blacks out of politics.

What is the Ku Klux Klan?

The Ku Klux Klan (KKK) began in 1866 near Pulaski, Tennessee, as a vigilante group of bored young Civil War veterans of Scotch-Irish descent. They created a secret lodge with mysterious titles and wore white robes and hoods as they rode around at night, drinking. But by early 1867, the Klan had become a highly organized movement active in several states, with the goal of keeping African Americans in their place. The Klan's methods ranged from subtle threats to blacks—and anyone who sympathized with them—to burning down homes. If these failed, the Klan was quite ready to use even more extreme violence. The Ku Klux Klan still exists today.

What other white hate groups existed?

The Citizens' Councils were another type of hate group in the South. Their goal was to control African Americans more through economic means than by violence. One Council leader said that their purpose was "to make it difficult, if not impossible, for any Negro who advocates desegregation to find and hold a job, get credit, or renew a mortgage."

Did anyone try to stop white hate groups?

Charges against white hate groups were hard to prove. Witnesses were afraid to testify, fearing that juries might be made up of Klansmen or their sympathizers. Although laws were passed against the KKK in the 1860s and 1870s in Congress and in the state capitals, Congress did not provide enough money or people to protect African Americans from this kind of violence, and often those charged with enforcing the laws were either on the side of the hate groups or too afraid to oppose them.

What role did religion play in the lives of the former slaves?

Unable to participate in political life and without decent jobs after the Civil War, many blacks turned to religion for comfort.

The Civil War also brought about a separation of white and black churches in the South. Most white southerners did not welcome African Americans into their church congregations. Those who did required blacks to sit in the areas where slaves had sat, and did not allow them to participate in the church's social or business affairs. As a result, in 1866 black Baptist congregations in South Carolina, Georgia, and Florida organized an association of their own. In 1880, a convention of black Baptist churches was held in Montgomery, Alabama. Black Presbyterians in the South also began to form their own churches. In 1870, the Colored Methodist Church in America was organized.

How did Reconstruction end?

In 1876, the results of the presidential election between Samuel J. Tilden, a Democrat, and Rutherford B. Hayes, a Republican, were disputed because of irregularities in the counting of votes. The two sides finally compromised: The Democrats agreed to the election of Hayes as president if he would guarantee that the states could rule themselves without federal interference. Known as the **Compromise of 1877,** the agreement allowed white majorities to regain control of state governments in the South. As a result, black voting rights were soon no longer protected, and the Reconstruction era was over.

Some Black Cowboys

Black cowboys drove cattle, scouted, and mined for gold. Nat Love, born into slavery in Tennessee in 1854, won a horse in a raffle at the age of fifteen. He rode it from his Texas home to Kansas, in the hope of becoming a cowboy. He made a name for himself by breaking the wildest horses, and became one of the best cowboys of his time. Love was an expert reader of brands, learned to speak Spanish, and won several roping and shooting contests. Because most of his feats took place in Deadwood, Dakota Territory, he earned the nickname "Deadwood Dick." He died in 1921.

Bill Pickett (1870–1932) was the most famous of the black rodeo cowboys. Born in Texas, he wrestled steers by using a technique he learned from watching bulldogs round up cattle: He would subdue the animal by biting its tender upper lip, then flip it on its side. He died in 1932 from a horse's kick to the head. In 1971, he became the first African American cowboy to be inducted into the National Cowboy Hall of Fame.

Louisiana; Philadelphia, Pennsylvania; New York City; and Memphis, Tennessee. Each of these cities had more than 40,000 black residents.

What was life like for African Americans in the cities after the turn of the century?

Blacks were attracted to the cities because of the opportunities for work, mostly in the iron and steel industries. They wrote letters back home to let friends and families know what opportunities were like:

> *The people are rushing here by the thousands, and I know that if you come here and rent a big house you can get all the roomers you want. I work in the Swift Packing Co., in the sausage department. My daughter and I work at the same place. We get $1.50 a day, and the hours are not so long, before you know it it is time to go home. I make $90 a month with ease. I am well and thankful to be in a city with no lynching and no beating.*

Occupations of Blacks in Chicago (1920)

Brick and stonemasons (126)

Building or general laborers (1,835)

Carpenters (275)

Clergymen (215)

Compositors and typesetters (113)

Coopers (148)

House painters (286)

Iron and steel workers (3,201)

Janitors (1,822)

Laborers (5,300)

Laborers, porters, and helpers in stores (1,210)

Lawyers (95)

Machinists (431)

Male servants (1,942)

Musicians or music teachers (254)

Non-store clerks (1,659)

Physicians (195)

Plumbers (105)

Porters in domestic or personal service (2,139)

Railway porters (2,540)

Semiskilled slaughter- and pack-inghouse workers (1,490)

Slaughter- and packinghouse laborers (1,242)

Tailors (371)

Waiters (2,315)

Newspapers and magazines published by African Americans appeared in all the larger black communities. Baptist and Pentecostal churches were established that appealed to African Americans who had newly arrived from the rural South. By the early twentieth century, many black communities had at least a few black businesspeople. African American fraternal orders, political organizations, social clubs, and newspapers helped to create feelings of racial pride.

Still, urban blacks had to deal with hostility from white workers. There was a lot of competition for jobs from European immigrants. African Americans were also excluded from labor unions.

What is the NAACP?

In 1905, a group of African Americans led by William Edward Burghardt (W. E. B.) Du Bois founded the Niagara Movement at Niagara Falls, Canada. The group was considered radical because it demanded action rather than empty promises. Members of the Niagara Movement later became part of the National Association for the Advancement of Colored People (**NAACP**), an interracial group founded in 1909. The NAACP used the legal system to fight racial discrimination, taking cases to courts through its Legal Defense Fund. The NAACP's goal was to inform people throughout the country of what was happening, both good and bad, to black people, and to help improve the lives of black people. Its many activities included providing details on every lynching it could to public officials and newspapers. The NAACP is still active today.

What is the National Urban League?

The National Urban League was formed as a result of the merging of three different organizations.

The National League for the Protection of Colored Women (NLPCW), founded in 1906 by white social worker Frances Kellor, worked to stop the exploitation of southern black women who had been lured north by "false representations regarding wages and employment."

The Committee for Improving the Industrial Condition of Negroes in New York (CIICN), also founded in 1906,

---

Famous Black Businesspeople of the Early Twentieth Century

In Birmingham, Alabama, Arthur George Gaston formed the Booker T. Washington Burial Society in 1923 to collect money from blacks to guarantee them a decent burial. He also founded the Booker T. Washington Business College in 1939, offering courses in bookkeeping, shorthand, and typing for blacks who could not attend white business schools. Gaston also started the Gaston Motel, and Citizens Federal Savings and Loan Association in 1957. In the 1960s he founded the A. G. Gaston Boy's Club.

Maggie Lena Walker (1867–1934), the daughter of a poor washerwoman, started the black-owned and -operated Saint Luke Penny Savings Bank in Richmond, Virginia, in 1903, becoming the first American woman to found a bank.

Sarah Breedlove McWilliams Walker (1867–1919), known as Madame C. J. Walker, the daughter of former slaves, invented a treatment for straightening kinky hair and began a million-dollar business promoting and selling her hair-care products.

Ida B. Wells Barnett

By the late 1880s and 1890s, whites were lynching African Americans throughout the country. Infuriated about the gains that blacks had made since slavery ended, white American mobs lynched blacks to assert white control. Men and women were lynched for talking fresh, for not addressing a white person correctly, and for testifying against a white person in court, for example.

In 1892, three African American men were lynched by a white mob in Memphis, Tennessee. Ida B. Wells Barnett (1862–1931), a black writer for the local black press, the *Free Speech* and *Headlights,* condemned the act and wrote passionately against it.

Wells Barnett went on to become the country's foremost anti-lynching crusader, lecturing throughout the country. She helped found the Anti-Lynching Committee in London, and became involved in the woman's suffrage movement as well.

encouraged African Americans to take vocational training and helped them to find jobs.

The Committee on Urban Conditions Among Negroes (CUCAN) was founded in 1910 by African American sociologist George Edmund Haynes and Ruth Standish (Mrs. William) Baldwin, a white social activist carrying on her late husband's work. Through research, counseling, and training, CUCAN helped black migrants from the rural South adjust to the realities of northern cities.

W. E. B. Du Bois

William Edward Burghardt (W. E. B.) Du Bois (1868–1963) was a writer, sociologist, philosopher, scholar, and leader respected throughout the world for his militant, outspoken support of justice and equal rights for blacks worldwide. He helped to organize the National Association for the Advancement of Colored People (NAACP) in 1909, and was editor of *Crisis,* the NAACP's magazine. He wrote over twenty books, the most popular of which was *The Souls of Black Folks* (1903). Criticized by those who disagreed with him and could not accept his ideas, he moved to Ghana, in West Africa, where he died on August 27, 1963.

Booker T. Washington

Booker T. Washington (1856–1915), born a slave, was an educator who believed that freedom for African Americans would come through personal education, self-help, and economic advancement rather than fighting for integration and equal rights. He advised blacks to take responsibility for their individual situations, and he opposed civil rights. Militant blacks disagreed with his views. In 1881 he was chosen to run Tuskegee Institute in Alabama, a new school for black students. Under his leadership, Tuskegee became a world famous center for agricultural research.

programs. Between 1910 and 1920, the Urban League helped to bring African Americans north and get decent employment for them. The Urban League was one of the first organizations to conduct and publish research to educate the country about the status of blacks.

Did any organizations support black businesses in the early 1900s?

Booker T. Washington founded the National Negro Business League in 1900. The organization provided a forum in which black businessmen could get encouragement and inspiration from one another. By 1915, the League had formed 600 state and local branches.

What white organizations or individuals helped African Americans in the early 1900s?

Financial support was offered by wealthy philanthropists who wanted to help the cause of black freedom. The John F. Slater Fund, established in 1882, supported schools, especially those that trained teachers. Between 1911 and 1932, Chicago humanitarian Julius Rosenwald contributed over $4,000,000 to help pay for the construction of school buildings in the rural South. The Phelps-Stokes Fund, founded in 1911, spent over half a million dollars during its first twenty-five years on activities to help blacks. The General Education Board, established by John D. Rockefeller in 1903, gave almost $700,000 to black edu-

A class meets at the Tuskegee Institute, 1902.

cation in its first ten years of existence. In 1903, Andrew Carnegie gave a grant of $600,000 to the Tuskegee Institute because of his respect for Booker T. Washington, the school's founder.

Arthur Schomburg, Collector

Arthur Schomburg (1874–1938), a journalist, lecturer, and businessman, spent his life collecting books, manuscripts, and artwork by and about black people—a rare passion at a time when few people were interested in black culture. In doing so, he played an enormous role in the preservation of African and African American culture.

In 1911, Schomburg helped found the Negro Society for Historical Research; in 1922, he presided over the American Negro Academy, founded to promote black art, science, and literature.

In 1926, the Carnegie Corporation purchased Schomburg's enormous collection and gave it to the New York Public Library. The collection has grown steadily over the years and is now the Schomburg Center for Research in Black Culture at the New York Public Library, the most important institution for research in African American life.

Because of Schomburg's interest and love for black life and art, we now have access to thousands of documents that inform us about our heritage.

Were blacks involved in politics at the turn of the century?

Booker T. Washington was highly respected by presidents William McKinley, William H. Taft, and Theodore Roosevelt. Because of Washington's recommendations, African Americans were appointed to several important positions in the federal and local Washington, D.C., governments. Robert H. Terrell was appointed to a municipal judgeship in the District of Columbia in 1902, and William H. Lewis was named assistant attorney general of the United States in 1911.

Black Fraternities

Alpha Phi Alpha (1906)

Kappa Alpha Psi (1911)

Omega Psi Phi (1911)

Phi Beta Sigma (1914)

About 2,000 blacks attended college in 1917.

How many African Americans were in college in the early 1900s?

Between 1900 and 1909, there were about 1,600 black college graduates. By 1915 that total had risen to more than 5,300. W. E. B. Du Bois referred to these college-educated blacks as the "Talented Tenth," although they made up much less than one-tenth of the African American population, which totaled about ten and a half million by 1920. Du Bois believe that African Americans would be "saved" by this small educated black elite.

In what activities did black college students participate in the early 1900s?

In 1905, nine African American college students at New York State's Cornell University decided to form a society for fellowship and mutual support. On October 23, 1906, the friends formed the first black **fraternity** (another word for "brotherhood"), Alpha Phi Alpha. There were many white fraternities already in existence. Over the next several years, additional black fraternal organizations were formed that mixed brotherhood with community work.

Black Sororities

Alpha Kappa Alpha (1908)

Delta Sigma Theta (1913)

Zeta Phi Beta (1920)

Sigma Gamma Rho (1922)

Black Nurses

The U.S. Army refused to enlist the hundreds of available black nurses because there was no separate housing for them. In 1918, after the war ended, the army finally called eighteen African American nurses to active duty, making them the first black women to officially enter the U.S. armed services.

What was World War I?

World War I lasted from 1914 to 1918. It began as a war between two European countries, Austria-Hungary and Serbia. The underlying causes of the conflict were rooted in European political and economic policies after 1871. Eventually, the war involved thirty-two countries. Twenty-eight of these countries were known as the Allies, and included Great Britain, France, Russia, and Italy. The other side, known as the Central Powers, included Germany, Austria-Hungary, the Ottoman Empire (present-day Turkey), and Bulgaria. The United States joined the war in 1917 on the side of the Allies.

Did African Americans fight in World War I?

There were 370,000 black soldiers and 1,400 black officers who served during World War I. A little more than half of these soldiers served in France.

African Americans were barred from the marines and could not become officers in the navy. Black officers and soldiers—even those with college degrees—were assigned to menial duties or labor battalions and were frequently humiliated by white officers. Bitter about their treatment, hundreds of black soldiers sent letters of complaint to Newton D. Baker, the secretary of war.

Were any African American soldiers honored for their service in World War I?

Despite their unfair treatment, the 369th Infantry Regiment, also known as the "Harlem Hell Fighters," had the best World War I record of any U.S Army regiment. Two members of the all-black 369th Infantry, Sergeant Henry Johnson and Needham Roberts, were awarded the French Croix de Guerre for aborting a German surprise attack. The two men killed or wounded more than twenty enemy soldiers.

In the 370th Infantry, black soldiers were awarded sixteen Distinguished Service Crosses and seventy-five Croix de Guerre medals. Having won honor and recognition on the battlefield, African Americans had mixed emotions about returning to the United States.

How did World War I affect blacks at home?

Improvements in transportation and communication had a huge impact on the daily lives of every American citizen, including blacks. Commercial radio broadcasting in the United States began in November 1920, providing people access to the news almost as soon as it happened. By 1924 there were 580 radio stations with thousands of listeners who could get their information before the next day's newspaper came.

The first talking movie, Al Jolson's *The Jazz Singer,* was released in 1927. By 1930, almost four-fifths of the American population was going to movies weekly.

The first car was built by Henry Ford in 1908. By the 1920s, cars (beginning with the Model T) were being mass-produced; therefore they were less expensive, and more people were able to buy them. While not many African Americans could afford cars at the time, many new businesses and jobs became available as a result of cars' widespread use. Roads had to be built. Tires and other auto parts were needed, as well as gasoline stations. People could travel farther, so there were more restaurants, theaters, and hotels. People could drive to their jobs, so they did not have to live in cities.

The black urban population expanded when blacks came to the cities to fill job openings created by the war. This in turn increased business and professional opportunities for African Americans. Blacks began to react to white racism with expressions of racial pride and unity. While educated African Americans did not agree on support for the war, they did agree that African Americans should use the war as an opportunity to make gains for black citizens.

How were race relations in the United States after World War I?

Both whites and blacks sought work after World War I. Because there were so few jobs, whites felt that their jobs were being taken away from them, and vice versa. When

During the Great Migration (1915–30), nearly one million African Americans left the South and resettled in the North.

Marcus Garvey's Enterprises

Garvey's weekly paper, *Negro World*, was published from 1918 to 1933 and became one of the leading African American periodicals. It sponsored beauty contests for black women, encouraged followers to support black businesses, and refused to carry advertisements for skin bleaches and hair straighteners.

In 1920, Garvey established the Negro Factories Corporation to build factories and produce goods for domestic and foreign sale to blacks. This corporation managed several UNIA businesses, including laundries, restaurants, a doll factory that manufactured black dolls for black children, tailoring and millinery establishments, and a printing press.

Garvey also established a black-owned steamship line, called the Black Star Line, which ran between the United States, the Caribbean, and Africa. But Garvey's three ships soon broke down and could not be used more than a few times. As a result, he lost $800,000 of the money invested by his black followers. By 1923, the Black Star Line was out of funds, and there were allegations that some of the company's funds had been deposited in the personal bank accounts of some of its officials. In January 1922 Garvey and three of the main officials of the Black Star Line were arrested and indicted for using the mails to defraud investors.

African Americans moved into any formerly white neighborhood, it caused tension, too.

In 1917, between forty and two hundred African Americans were killed in East Saint Louis, Illinois, by a white mob that invaded the black community. That same year, sixty-three black soldiers in Houston, Texas, were court-martialed and thirteen hanged without appeal after a black battalion rioted in reaction to white harassment.

During the Summer of 1919, more than twenty violent race riots occurred in the United States, including disturbances in Longview, Texas; Washington, D.C.; Chicago, Illinois; Knoxville, Tennessee; and Omaha, Nebraska. These events motivated African Americans to defend their rights and support outspoken leaders.

Who was Marcus Garvey?

Marcus Garvey (1887–1940) a Jamaican immigrant (someone who moves to another country voluntarily), was

What was the Harlem Renaissance? ◆ What caus
he Harlem Renaissance? ◆ Why was it called
Harlem Renaissance? ◆ Were there Harl
Renaissance artists outside of Harlem? ◆ Did
Harlem Renaissance artists work on the subject
subject of being black? ◆ How did the write
artists and performers of the Harlem Renaissa
become famous? ◆ Who were some of the writ
of the Harlem Renaissance? ◆ Who were some
he other creative people of the Harl
Renaissance? ◆ When did the Harlem Renaissa

The Harlem Renaissance

What was the Harlem Renaissance?

The **Harlem Renaissance,** also called the Black Renaissance and the New Negro Movement, was a time in the 1920s when a large number of black poets, writers, artists, musicians, and performers expressed themselves and their experiences as blacks in America through their writing, art, and music. Black artists were able to educate the public about being black in America and to show new pride in being black.

What caused the Harlem Renaissance?

World War I had just ended, and people, both black and white, were experiencing new feelings and attitudes and were interested in trying new things. Black migrants left the South to start new lives in the North, where they saw black organizations, businesses, and publications growing everywhere. African Americans were beginning to look at themselves and celebrate their differences, instead of merely copying white ways. There was a growing interest in "the Negro": People, black and white, were curious about black music (jazz, spirituals), stories, and culture. Feelings of racial pride were emerging, and the time was right for new voices to be heard. The arts began to reflect these changes.

Why was it called the Harlem Renaissance?

Renaissance means "rebirth." In the 1920s, black artists flocked to Harlem, a section of New York City that also attracted immigrants from Barbados, Haiti, Puerto Rico, Cuba, and other Caribbean countries. Harlem was a black city within a city: exciting, modern, with many nationalities, languages, and cultures. It attracted young black artists and intellectuals from all over the United States and foreign countries. There they worked among their people and tried to represent their race accurately in all art forms. They stunned and dazzled white and black audiences and critics alike with their work. They took the pain and suffering of a whole race and turned it into art. Harlem was considered the center of the renaissance.

When did the Harlem Renaissance begin?

No one agrees on exactly when the Harlem Renaissance began, but everyone acknowledges that it reached its peak in the 1920s.

Some consider Alain Locke (1886–1954), a philosophy professor at Howard University, the father of the Harlem Renaissance. His book *The New Negro,* published in 1925, contained numerous poems, essays, stories, and art that clearly demonstrated the profound influence that black culture had on America. His book spread the exciting news of

Zora Neale Hurston

Born in Florida in 1903, Zora Neale Hurston studied at Morgan State, Barnard College, and Howard University. While at Howard, she published some short stories for *Opportunity* and was influenced by the black intellectual Alain Locke. She earned her degree in anthropology from Barnard (she was the first black woman to attend) and utilized this interest in folklore to write movingly and accurately about black life in the rural South.

Mules and Men, published in 1935, is a book of southern black folktales; *Their Eyes Were Watching God* (1937) is a classic work. Her autobiography, *Dust Tracks on the Road* (1942), is also widely acclaimed.

Like many writers of the Harlem Renaissance, Hurston's stories went largely unrecognized until after her death. She died penniless in 1960.

the Harlem Renaissance to the rest of America and the world. He was among several important black intellectuals who promoted African and African American culture.

How did the writers, artists, and performers of the Harlem Renaissance become famous?

Their work was published in black journals, often with the help of white patrons and black editors, such as Charles S. Johnson at *Opportunity* (published by the Urban League); A. Philip Randolph, editor of the *Messenger*; and Jessie Fauset (1886–1961) and W. E. B. Du Bois at *Crisis* (published by the NAACP).

Were there Harlem Renaissance artists outside of Harlem?

The Harlem Renaissance affected the whole world. Blacks everywhere became inspired, and started poetry circles, little theaters, and painting classes. Although New York City was the center of the Harlem Renaissance, there were many creative blacks in other cities: in Boston, William Stanley Braithwaite (1878–1962), a poet; and in Washington, D.C., writers Georgia Douglas Johnson (1886–1966) William Cuney, and Sterling Brown (1901–   ). Alain Locke, also of Washington, was a writer and professor of philosophy at Howard University.

Did the Harlem Renaissance artists' work only cover the subject of being black?

Black writers and artists of the Harlem Renaissance did not want to write like other writers had. They agreed that their work might have a racial theme, but would be for both black and nonblack audiences. Previous black writing featured grinning characters who spoke poor English, but the new writers did not want to write that way. More books were published by black authors during the 1920s than any other decade in American history.

What was the best literary work of the Harlem Renaissance period?

Jean Toomer (1894–1967) wrote several poems exploring black experience; but his novel *Cane,* published in

1923, is widely considered one of the best literary works of the Harlem Renaissance.

Cane, a lyrical novel of symbolic, mystical sketches and poems, explores the lifestyles of the black poor in a white America. Many critics consider *Cane* a masterpiece— among the best novels ever written by a black.

Who were some other novelists of the Harlem Renaissance?

Jessie Fauset (1894–1967), who was also an editor of *Crisis,* wrote novels about respectable members of the educated black middle class who had to deal with problems involving race. Her book *There is Confusion* (1924) was the first Harlem Renaissance novel by a woman.

Rudolf Fisher (1897–1934) was a doctor and an intellectual who also contributed much to the Harlem Renaissance. He wrote stories and novels about life in Harlem, and his *Conjure Man Dies: A Mystery Tale of Dark Harlem* (1932) is considered the first detective story written by a black American. It is a murder mystery that takes place in Harlem.

Other black novelists include Zora Neale Hurston (1903–1960), Langston Hughes (1902–1967), James Weldon Johnson (1871–1938), and Claude McKay (1890–1948).

Who were some of the Harlem Renaissance's best poets?

Although they also wrote novels, Claude McKay and Langston Hughes were probably most famous for their poetry.

Claude McKay was born in Jamaica, and in 1913 he arrived in America to study agriculture at Tuskegee Institute. His interest in writing brought him to New York City, the center of book and magazine publishing. He eventually became an editor of *The Liberator,* where he published "If we must die" (1919), a powerful poem of social protest; he also wrote "The lynching," another passionate poem. In 1922 he published one of the most significant works of the period, *Harlem Shadows,* a collection of poems. His novels include *Home to Harlem* (1928) and *Banjo* (1929). McKay was the first black writer of the 1920s to attract a large white audience.

Harlem. He wrote with compassion and passion about what it meant to be black, while celebrating the creative powers of African American culture. Although Hughes was also a novelist, essayist, children's book author, and librettist, he was primarily known for his work in poetry. Hughes, the "Poet Laureate of Harlem," is one of the most beloved and popular black writers of all time.

Were there any other poets of the Harlem Renaissance?

Another well-known poet to emerge from this period was Countee Cullen (1903–1946). Cullen was orphaned while very young and was adopted by a prominent pastor of a Methodist Church in New York.

He was praised for his poems when he was only in high school, and he published his first book, *Color*, in 1925. Two years later, he published *The Ballad of the Brown Girl* and *Copper Sun*, followed by *The Black Christ* in 1929. He won

"Just a Little Blackbird"

Florence Mills, born in Washington, D.C., in 1895, fell in love with performing at an early age. She participated in many amateur shows and debuted in *Sons of Ham* when she was just five years old. In 1910, she moved to New York and formed an act with her sisters called the Mills Trio, and they performed in vaudeville shows.

After several years in Chicago, Mills returned to New York, where she received her big break—she replaced one of the leads in Broadway's *Shuffle Along*. The twenty-six-year-old quickly captivated audiences, and she went on to become the most popular entertainer of the Harlem Renaissance. She performed in London, where her breathtaking dancing was praised as high art. In New York in 1924, she starred in *From Dixie to Broadway*, where she sang her trademark song, "I'm just a Little Blackbird Lookin' for a Bluebird."

Mills eventually became dedicated to creating her own all-black musical revue, and even turned down a role with the popular all-white Ziegfeld Follies dance troupe. Mills' dream was achieved with *Blackbirds of 1926*, which ran in Harlem, London, and Paris.

When she died in 1927 at the age of thirty-one, the streets of Harlem were crowded with fans mourning the loss of the much-loved star.

several awards for his poems, and he also wrote children's stories and one novel, *One Way to Heaven.*

Cullen stressed his desire to be known not just as a black poet, but as a poet.

What was happening in theater during the 1920s Harlem Renaissance period?

In the musical Runnin' Wild (1923), the famous dance the Charleston was introduced.

In 1921, an all-black musical opened on Broadway in New York City. The lyrics were written by Noble Sissle (1889–1975) and Eubie Blake (1883–1983), and the play was called *Shuffle Along.* The energetic music and lively, wild dancing style of this musical comedy was well-known to the black community, but it was new to most white audiences. *Shuffle Along* marked the first time that African Americans were able to show real African American song, dance, and humor to all of New York City, and eventually to the whole country.

Shuffle Along was the reason why many black performers became famous. Florence Mills (1895–1927) became very popular from her role as one of the lead singers, and Josephine Baker (1906–1975) and Paul Robeson (1898–1976) also started their careers with *Shuffle Along.*

Another exciting performer of the 1920s was Bill "Bojangles" Robinson (1878–1949). He performed in several

Josephine Baker

When Josephine Baker was a teenager, she performed as a chorus girl in the successful musical comedy *Shuffle Along.* From there she landed other parts in shows, but it wasn't until she went to Paris that she became a sensation.

She appeared in *La Revue Negre,* where she performed outrageous and daring dances. The audiences adored her, and she went on to perform in the Folies Bergere, where she performed her most unforgettable work. Baker became known for her eccentric, lively performances and her wild dances. She eventually moved into film and light opera.

During World War II, she worked as a spy for the French Resistance, and she was awarded a medal for her bravery. When she returned to the United States, Baker refused to perform in segregated venues and spoke out against discrimination.

bringing African-influenced styles to the stage. In 1933, Helmsley Winfield performed in *Emperor Jones*, becoming the first African American to dance for the Metropolitan Opera.

Mulatto, a play written by Langston Hughes, ran for 375 consecutive shows.

What music were people listening to during the Harlem Renaissance?

Jazz was the most popular music of this period, and it played an enormous role in the vital cultural scene in Harlem. Some say that jazz is the most unique form of creative expression of our times.

By the 1920s, jazz had spread throughout the country and the world. Many jazz performers came to Harlem, where they performed for black and white audiences. Affluent whites came from downtown New York City to Harlem clubs, where they heard such star musicians as Louis "Satchmo" Armstrong (1901–1971), Edward "Duke" Ellington (1899–1974), and Fletcher Henderson (1897–1952). For many people, jazz expressed a breaking away

Ladies Who Sang the Blues...and Jazz

Gertrude "Ma" Rainey (1886–1939). Known as the "Mother of the Blues." Performed with her husband, singer/dancer William "Pa" Rainey. Recorded the classic "See See Rider Blues" with Louis Armstrong; also recorded with Coleman Hawkins and Fletcher Henderson.

Bessie Smith (1894–1937). Known as "The Empress of the Blues." Her first record, "Down-Hearted Blues," sold more than one million copies in 1923. At one point she was the highest paid black entertainer in the country. Made a classic recording of "St. Louis Blues" with Louis Armstrong. Other popular songs include "Gimmee a Pigfoot," "Empty Bed Blues," and "Nobody Knows You When You're Down and Out." Her sense of timing and drama, along with her rich voice, make her highly appealing to lovers of jazz, too.

Billie Holiday (1915–1959). Known as "Lady Day." Considered one of the best jazz singers of all time. Recorded with Benny Goodman in 1933 and performed with Artie Shaw and Count Basie. Some of her recordings include torch songs such as "My Man" and "Don't Explain," and classics such as "Strange Fruit," "God Bless the Child," and "Good Morning, Heartache."

Satchmo

Louis "Satchmo" Armstrong holds a very important place in jazz history. He played all over the world, recorded several best-selling records, and influenced a host of musicians, vocalists, and bandleaders with his pioneering work. Many people call him the most influential and creative musician of this century.

Louis Armstrong was born in a shack in New Orleans. When he was a teenager, he got a job delivering coal in the area where the "hot blues" (soon to be known as jazz), was beginning. He began to play for money and soon befriended Joseph "King" Oliver (1885–1938), who eventually asked Satchmo to join him in his Creole Jazz Band in Chicago. By the 1930s, Armstrong was playing the trumpet, singing, leading bands, and recording some of the most important music in the history of jazz.

Satchmo revolutionized the role of the voice in the song; he saw the voice as an instrument that was as important as his playing. Some of his most important jazz recordings include "Dippermouth Blues," "Heebie Jeebies," "Hotter Than That," and Fats Wallers' "Ain't Misbehavin'." He also became popular for his recordings of some popular songs such as "Hello Dolly," "Mack the Knife," and "What a Wonderful World."

from tradition. Listeners felt liberated by the fresh, exciting sounds of jazz.

Another style of music that became popular in the 1920s was blues. The blues has a long, rich history. It probably evolved from work songs, spirituals, and the call-and-

What Is Jazz?

Before 1900, black musicians in New Orleans (a city with a rich international heritage) were playing upbeat music that was called "hot blues," and that eventually came to be known as jazz. Jazz came about from the mixing of several types of music: spirituals, blues, ragtime, and gospel. It was spontaneous music; musicians played around with different styles, adding their own original ideas to a basic musical framework in a process known as improvisation.

Many people consider jazz to be the most unique form of creative expression ever to come out of American culture. It continues to be popular today.

Famous Writers, Artists, and Musicians of the Harlem Renaissance

James Weldon Johnson (1871–1938). Novelist, poet, and composer. He was also Florida's first black attorney, and the first field secretary of the NAACP. He wrote and arranged Negro spirituals with his brother J. Rosamond Johnson.

Aaron Douglas (1899–1979). Illustrator and muralist.

Lois Mailou Jones (1905–). Painter and designer.

J. Rosamond Johnson (1873–1954). Composer. Wrote and arranged black spirituals with his brother James Weldon Johnson. His most famous work is "Lift Ev'ry Voice and Sing," also known as the Negro National Anthem.

Nella Larsen (1891–1964) Novelist. Her novels include *Quicksand* (1928) and *Passing* (1929).

Augusta Savage (1900–1962). Sculptor. Her work was represented at the first all-black art exhibits in America, sponsored by the Harmon Foundation in New York City. The first black to win acceptance into the National Association of Women Painters and Sculptors. Significant works include *Lift Every Voice and Sing, Gamin, Marcus*

Garvey, and *W. E. B. Du Bois.*

Ferdinand "Jelly Roll" Morton (1891–1941). Pianist, composer, and bandleader. His "Jelly Roll Blues" (1919) was the first published jazz piece; he is considered the first jazz composer. In 1923, he recorded with the New Orleans Rhythm Kings; this made him the first African American to record with a white band.

Fletcher Henderson (1887–1952). Pianist and bandleader. His big band was the first big band to play jazz. Played at the Roseland Ballroom on Broadway for eight years. Performed with Bessie Smith, Louis Armstrong, and Coleman Hawkins.

Clara Smith (1895–1935). Blues and vaudeville singer. Known as "Queen of the Moaners."

Roland Hayes (1897–1977). Singer. In 1917, he became the first black to give a recital at Boston's Symphony Hall. In 1924 he won the prestigious Spingarn Medal.

Wallace Thurman (1902–1934). Journalist, editor, and novelist. Edited the radical *Fire!*. Novels include *The Blacker the Berry* and *Infants of Spring.*

When did the Harlem Renaissance end?

The black cultural awakening of the 1920s slowed down in the 1930s as the worldwide economic depression diverted people's attention from cultural to economic matters. The Great Depression made it harder for artists and writers to earn money. Many of them found it impossible to stay off relief, but for some the Roosevelt administration's national recovery programs (the New Deal) allowed them to continue working while receiving a check from the government. The Harlem Renaissance really never ended; it opened the door for talented black artists for generations to come.

THE DEPRESSION, THE NEW DEAL, AND WORLD WAR II

What was the Great Depression?

On October 29, 1929, the U.S. stock market crashed. This meant that the value of stocks went way down, because everyone sold their stocks in a panic. This stock market panic was caused by many factors, including risky investments and overproduction of products. The crash resulted in the Great Depression, which spread over the United States and became worldwide in the early 1930s.

How did the Great Depression affect blacks?

The depression affected everyone. Many businesses went bankrupt, banks failed, and more than 12 million people lost their jobs. Among African Americans, unemployment and poverty were already high. During the depression, blacks helped one another by selling dinners and homemade liquor and by holding rent parties where each guest would pay a few cents to get in, which would go toward helping the host pay the rent.

How were African Americans in the South affected by the Great Depression?

American farmers were the first group to be affected by the Great Depression. The farmers in the South did not have the money to buy seeds or supplies or even the goods that they helped to produce.

Most blacks in the South worked as farm laborers. When farmers started losing money, the black farm labor-

Black Athletes Boosting Black Morale

In 1936, at the Berlin Olympics, Jesse Owens (1913–1980) won four gold medals in track and field, at that time the most universally acclaimed feat in the history of the games. When Adolf Hitler, the German Nazi dictator, refused to present him the medals he had won in the various competitions, Owens became even more famous because of the publicity.

On June 22, 1937, Joe Louis (1914–1981) defeated James J. Braddock to become the heavyweight boxing champion of the word. Black America vigorously celebrated this exciting victory, praising Louis as a symbol of black strength and power.

On April 15, 1947, Jackie Robinson began his major league baseball career with the Brooklyn Dodgers, becoming the first black player in organized professional baseball, opening the door for other black baseball players and black athletes in all sports.

ers lost their jobs. There was no work. They couldn't move to the North, as many had done in the past, either; by that point whites were working in the jobs that had previously been filled by blacks from the South. For these reasons, southern blacks were probably the most economically troubled group during the Great Depression.

How did blacks and whites join to seek better social conditions?

The Communist party was one political organization that made a special effort to attract African Americans, especially those in the inner cities. Based on a political system begun in Russia, Communism is a system in which the main resources and means of production are owned by the state instead of by individuals. The party staged marches, organized boycotts of businesses that did not hire blacks, and helped people that had been evicted from their homes. Some famous members of the Communist party were the actor Paul Robeson and the novelist Richard Wright. In 1932, 1936, and 1940 the party even ran a black candidate, James Ford, for vice president. But the party failed to attract a big enough following among African Americans.

Blacks also became involved in labor unions, such as the all-black Brotherhood of Sleeping Car Porters.

What are unions?

A union (short for trade or labor union) is an association of workers established to improve economic and civil rights changes. During the 1930s, for example, the NAACP began a legal battle against segregation in public schools. In 1938, it gained a victory when the U.S. Supreme Court ordered the University of Missouri law school to enroll a black man. The NAACP also played an important role in the Scottsboro case.

What was the Scottsboro case?

The Scottsboro case was a legal case involving two white girls who accused nine black boys—aged twelve to nineteen—from Scottsboro, Alabama, of rape in March 1931. The nine—Clarence Norris, Olen Montgomery, Andrew Wright, Willie Roberson, Ozie Powell, Eugene Williams, Charley Weems, Roy Wright, and Haywood Patterson—became known as the Scottsboro Boys, and were tried and convicted by an all-white jury. At the trial the evidence against them consisted mostly of the testimony of the girls involved. Even though one of the girls admitted she had been lying, eight of the boys were sentenced to death. The ninth, who was thirteen years old, was sentenced to life imprisonment. Many Americans, black and

Haywood Patterson wrote his account of the trial and its aftermath in the book Scottsboro Boy, published in 1950.

One of the Scottsboro Boys. *A.P./Worldwide Photos*

Mary McLeod Bethune

After graduating from Moody Bible Institute in 1895 (where she had been the only black student), Mary McLeod Bethune (1875–1955) taught at Haines Institute in Georgia. In 1904 she traveled to Daytona Beach, Florida, to establish a school for young black women, despite having only $1.50 in her pocket. Using money raised from selling sweet potato pies and donations from churches and clubs, she created the Daytona Normal and Industrial Institute for Negro Girls. In 1923, she merged her school with another black Florida school, the Cookman Institute, to form Bethune-Cookman College, which still exists today. Bethune also founded the National Council of Negro Women (NCNW) in 1935, was the director of the National Urban League, and served as an adviser to four presidents.

white, were shocked and considered the verdict racist. Many organizations, including the Communist party and the NAACP, supported the Scottsboro Boys, and their case became international news.

After six years of appeals and retrials—during which the U.S. Supreme Court twice declared mistrials—the indictments were dropped against five of the men. The remaining four received long prison terms, but all were paroled by 1946 except Patterson, who escaped to Michigan.

What was the Tuskegee Experiment?

In 1932, the U.S. government's public health service division began studying a disease called syphilis in Alabama near the Tuskegee Institute.

The white doctors used African American men as their research subjects. All of these men were poor. Some had the disease, others didn't. (The men with the syphilis called what they had "bad blood.") The men with the "bad blood" were told that they were getting free treatment from the U.S. government; however, the doctors were not treating the men with the disease at all. They were really just observing how the syphilis affected the men until death. The black men had been deceived.

The National Youth Administration (NYA), established in 1935, was a student work program that involved 64,000 young African Americans. Mary McLeod Bethune (1875–1955) was appointed to head its Division of Negro Affairs.

In the Civilian Conservation Corps (CCC), established in 1933, unemployed young men from the cities were put to work in rural areas. There they built roads, worked on projects designed to prevent soil erosion, and planted trees during reforestation programs. This program employed 200,000 young blacks.

The **Work Projects Administration (WPA)** employed approximately a million African Americans in jobs ranging from clerical work to bridge building to mural painting in post offices. The WPA promoted black adult education, hired unemployed black professionals, and stimulated the arts within the black community. The education program employed more than 5,000 African Americans as leaders and supervisors, taught nearly 250,000 African Americans to read and write, and trained many for skilled jobs. Harry Hopkins, head of the WPA, helped establish policies making it illegal for any relief official to discriminate on the basis of race, creed, or color.

Some Black Artists

Horace Pippin (1881–1946). Painter. Self-taught artist who started painting in 1920. Many of his early works were burned into wood panels with a hot poker. Portrayed scenes from World War I, during which he became partially paralyzed. His work was shown in 1938 at an exhibit entitled "Masters of Popular Painting—Artists of the People" at the Museum of Modern Art in New York City. Some of his works include *John Brown Goes to a Hanging* and *The End of the War: Starting Home.*

Jacob Lawrence (1917–). Painter. Painted vivid, small panels telling stories about American history. His *Migration Stories* depicted blacks from the South migrating to the urban areas of the North with hopes of a better life; these scenes showed crowds of African Americans in the streets, on trains, in bus stations, etc. In 1942, he became the first African American artist to have his work acquired by the Museum of Modern Art in New York City. Won the Spingarn Medal in 1970. Also documented the lives of Harriet Tubman, John Brown, and Toussaint L'Ouverture.

How did the New Deal programs affect African Americans in the arts?

The Federal Writers' Project (FWP) gave young black

The Federal Theater Project

President Roosevelt's New Deal agency, the Works Progress Administration (WPA), did much to promote black participation in the American arts in the 1930s. One of the programs sponsored by the WPA was the Federal Theater Project. This project enabled more than 800 African Americans to act in circuses, vaudeville comedies, children's theatrical performances, and in dramatic theater. It also created many opportunities for blacks to act in plays that depicted black life. These plays included Hall Johnson's *Run Little Chillun*, Rudolf Fisher's *Conjure Man Dies: A Mystery Tale of Dark Harlem*, and an adaptation of Shakespeare's *Macbeth* set in Haiti.

Many of the performers in the Federal Theater Project went on to become film and Broadway stars—including the dancer Katherine Dunham and the actor Rex Ingram (1895–1969).

By 1941, there were about 150,000 African American federal employees.

writers and scholars such as Horace R. Cayton, St. Clair Drake, Ralph Ellison, Zora Neale Hurston, and Richard Wright job opportunities and training. The Federal Music Project staged concerts including the works of black composers; the Federal Art Project employed hundreds of black artists; and the Federal Theater Project established a black unit that employed about 500 blacks in New York, developed dramatic productions on black life and history, and carried shows to black communities throughout the country.

Native Son

Native Son, written by Richard Wright (1908–1960) and published in 1940, was the story of a young black man who murdered a white woman. It showed the horror and hatred that could be caused by poverty. The first book by a black person to become a Book-of-the-Month Club selection, it helped to inspire the next generation of black writers.

Did the New Deal programs help solve the economic problems of African Americans?

Poor blacks were able to get financial relief and affordable housing. They also benefited economically from new jobs that were created and from the minimum wage laws. African Americans were also hired to build the new government-financed housing.

Eleanor Roosevelt, President Roosevelt's wife, convinced him to

What was World War II?

World War II was the most destructive war in human history. It began in 1939 when Germany invaded Poland, but eventually grew to include most of the countries of the world. In Europe, Germany fought England and the Union of Soviet Socialist Republics (USSR); in the Pacific, the United States fought Japan. The most horrible atrocity of the war was the systematic, racist killing of 6 million Jews by the German Nazis in Europe. Some 45 million people lost their lives in the war, which ended in 1945, leaving a new world order dominated by the United States and the USSR.

What role did African Americans play in World War II?

The U.S. Army and Navy remained segregated during World War II. The War Department eventually approved the training of black officers, and allowed blacks to serve as pilots and in medical and engineering units. Approximately half a million blacks served overseas in segregated units in the Pacific and Europe, but in many cases racial conflicts took place both on military posts and in occupied zones abroad, and at camps where black soldiers protested against poor conditions and discrimination.

Who were the Tuskegee Airmen?

The 332nd Fighter Group, known as the Tuskegee Airmen because they were graduates of the segregated pilot training program at Tuskegee, Alabama, set records for their aerial expertise in World War II. During more than 200 missions as heavy bomber escorts, they never lost an escorted plane to enemy fighters; and they managed to sink a German navy destroyer with aircraft gunfire. These accomplishments are still unmatched.

The Blood Expert

Charles Drew (1904–1950), a physician, was an expert on blood. His breakthrough research in plasma and blood preservation led to the establishment in New York City of the first successful blood bank. Great Britain called upon him to create donor banks for soldiers during World War II, and he did the same for the American Red Cross in the United States. His hard work saved the lives of tens of thousands of soldiers during the war.

The Summer 1943 Race Riots

In the summer of 1943, a riot started when blacks were promoted at a Mobile, Alabama, shipyard. The National Guard was called out to maintain order. In a Beaumont, Texas, riot on June 16, two persons were killed and martial law was declared. In Detroit, twenty-five blacks and nine whites were killed before federal troops restored order. In August, there was a riot in Harlem.

How did World War II affect the economic status of African Americans?

Established under President Roosevelt's Executive Order Number 8802, the Committee on Fair Employment Practice encouraged African Americans to move to cities such as Detroit and Los Angeles, where there were jobs in defense plants. This migration more than tripled the black population in the western states.

As more African Americans moved from the rural South to the cities, their economic status improved. Before 1948, 78 percent of blacks earned under $3,000 a year. Between 1948 and 1961, that percentage decreased to 47 percent. At the same time, the percentage of African Americans earning over $10,000 a year, previously less than 1 percent, increased to 17 percent. There was also an increase in the number of blacks attending college. In 1947, there were 124,000 black college students; in 1961, there were 233,000.

Blacks were still struggling to obtain dignity. In the South, married adult blacks were still not called Mr. or Mrs. by whites.

What books on the black experience became popular at this time?

Books published during the 1930s and 1940s helped the larger population understand the black experience. These included Richard Wright's novel *Native Son* (1940); *Black Metropolis* (1945), an important sociological study, by St. Clair Drake and Horace Cayton; *An American Dilemma: The Negro Problem and Modern Democracy* (1944), by the Swedish economist Gunnar Myrdal; and *From Slavery to Freedom* (1947) by the historian John Hope Franklin.

What role did African Americans play in politics after World War II?

The growing number of educated and affluent blacks in the cities made major political gains possible. Black

Adam Clayton Powell Jr.

Adam Clayton Powell Jr. (1908–1972) was one of the most controversial and flamboyant figures in American politics. He began speaking out for the oppressed from the pulpit of the Abyssinian Baptist Church in Harlem, where his father had been pastor. In 1941, he became New York's first black city councilman, helped by the 14,000 members of his congregation. Three years later he was elected to the House of Representatives, where, boldly, he personally integrated the dining rooms, showers, and barbershops that black congressmen were not allowed to use. Because of him, black reporters were admitted to the House press gallery, blacks were admitted to the U.S. Naval Academy, and blacks were able to serve on the U.S. delegation to the United Nations. He drafted bills to end discriminatory practices such as poll taxes and sponsored legislation advocating a minimum wage scale.

But Powell was soon accused of putting his friends on the congressional payroll. He was also frequently absent from congressional votes, and lived what some considered the life of a playboy. In 1967 the House condemned him, and he moved to the Caribbean island of Bimini. In 1970 he lost the New York Democratic primary for his congressional seat, and retired officially. He died in Miami in 1972.

urban voters heavily supported liberal Democratic candidates. In 1954, three blacks—Augustus Hawkins of California, Adam Clayton Powell Jr. of New York, and William L. Dawson of Illinois—were elected to the U.S. House of Representatives, the largest number since Reconstruction.

What was the Civil Rights Movement? ◆ What w
he Brown v. Boar— Education case about? ◆ D
he Supreme Court rul— Brown v. Board
ducation end school segregation immediately?
ow — the civil rights —ement begin? ◆ How
—e —ack — —thing kn— w— — —ri— th
ontgomery bus boycott? ◆ Was the Montgome
us boy— — first tim— a bus compan— —ad be—
oycot— —v— —eg—ti—n — —a— —e —o—gomer
us boycott a success? ◆ What happened to Ro—
arks after the Montgomery bus boycott? ◆ Wh—

THE CIVIL RIGHTS MOVEMENT

What was the civil rights movement?

Civil rights are the rights each citizen has to equal protection under the law and equal opportunity to participate completely in national life, regardless of race, religion, or sex.

But during the first half of the twentieth century, especially in the South, segregation was practiced in most areas of American life. Blacks and whites could not attend the same school, or eat at the same table in a restaurant, or marry someone not of their race. Because of poll taxes and unfair literacy tests, most African Americans were prevented from voting.

During the 1950s and 1960s, black leaders used the courts, mass marches and demonstrations, nonviolent resistance, and the press to get racist laws erased. These efforts have come to be known as the civil rights movement.

What was the Brown v. Board of Education case about?

In the 1940s and 1950s, according to the laws of most southern states, there were separate schools for blacks and whites, from elementary school through college. Linda Brown was a seven-year-old black girl who lived in Topeka, Kansas, in 1950. There were two schools in the town: one for black children, which was far from her home, and one for white children, which was four blocks

A white girl and a black girl examine each other after their Fort Myer, Virginia, school was desegregated in September 1954.

Thurgood Marshall headed the Legal Defense and Educational Fund, created by the NAACP to battle discriminatory laws in the United States.

from her home. Linda's father did not see why she should have to travel when there was a perfectly good school that was closer. He decided to go to court to fight for Linda's right to attend the closer school. His lawsuit, called *Brown v. Board of Education of Topeka, Kansas,* was handled by Thurgood Marshall, chief attorney for the NAACP (and future associate justice of the Supreme Court). The case went all the way to the Supreme Court of the United States. The Court ruled that segregated public schools in the United States were unconstitutional. Every victory in cases such as *Brown v. Board of Education* made African Americans more confident that justice was possible through use of the judicial system.

Did the Supreme Court ruling in Brown v. Board of Education end school segregation immediately?

Most states did not want to accept the ruling. Besides, the Supreme Court's decision did not include instructions on how the ruling was to be put into practice. Desegregation

The Little Rock Nine

In September 1957, nine black teenagers—Jefferson Thomas, Carlotta Walls, Gloria Ray, Elizabeth Eckford, Thelma Mothershed, Melba Pattillo, Terrance Roberts, Minniejean Brown, and Ernest Green—tried to enroll at Central High School, an all-white school, in Little Rock, Arkansas. The governor called the Arkansas National Guard to prevent them from entering. Mobs of angry whites outside the school threatened the students, their supporters, and even newspaper reporters.

Daisy Bates, president of the Arkansas chapter of the NAACP, offered her home and her services to help the students, who became known as the Little Rock Nine. The students met at her home every day, and she arranged for them to be taken to the school. Because of her connection with the students her home was bombed, shot at, and stoned, and crosses were burned on her lawn. People or businesses who sold or advertised in the *Arkansas State Press,* the newspaper owned by Bates and her husband, were threatened, until the paper was forced to close. It was the family's only source of income.

The mobs at Central High School became an international story. On the first day the students entered the school, the mob rushed the school. The police made no attempt to stop them, and the nine black students had to make a daring escape by car from an underground garage.

Minniejean Brown was suspended from Central when she poured chili on the head of a white boy who kept calling her racist names in the cafeteria. After she did so, there was absolute silence. Then the cafeteria workers, all black, applauded.

Ernest Green, who entered as a senior, was the first and only one of the Little Rock Nine to graduate that June. Martin Luther King Jr. was a guest at the ceremony, and sat with Green's mother and Daisy Bates. When Green's name was called, there was silence instead of applause as there had been for the other students. "But I figured they didn't have to," said Green. "Because after I got that diploma, that was it. I had accomplished what I had come there for."

began almost immediately in Washington, D.C., and Baltimore, while Texas integrated only one school district, Arkansas only two, and in the rest of the South, not a single classroom was racially mixed. Most of the states waited for specific instructions from the Court on how to end school segregation. A year after the *Brown* decision, the Court was still silent. Instead, the justices asked the federal courts closer to the local school districts to make sure their districts admitted black children to public schools "with all deliberate speed."

It took many years for all-white schools to allow black students to attend. When they finally had to, violence often marked the first day that the first black student entered, or tried to enter, an all-white school.

How did the civil rights movement begin?

Although people had been working for civil rights for African Americans for some time, one famous event is considered the beginning of the civil rights movement.

In the South of the 1950s, public transportation was segregated. On buses, white people rode in the front and black people rode in the back. There were signs on the buses reading WHITE FORWARD, COLORED REAR. If all of the WHITE seats were filled and more white people got on, any

Charlayne Hunter

Charlayne Hunter-Gault is known to millions of Americans as the national correspondent for the Public Broadcasting System's (PBS) *MacNeil/ Lehrer News Hour.* In January 1961, she was one of two black students to enter the University of Georgia, which had been ordered by a federal court to desegregate. When the two arrived at the school, they found that their registration process had been halted by a local judge. They left, but a few hours later the ruling was overturned. They went back to the university to complete their registration.

The night before the first day of classes, a noisy, angry mob gathered outside Charlayne's dormitory. A brick and a bottle were thrown through her window. She later learned that all the other students had been told to turn off the lights in their rooms when it got dark, making Charlayne's brightly lit windows an easy target. As the crowd got uglier, Charlayne and the other black student were forced to leave the campus for their own safety. But on Friday, a judge ordered the university to admit them no later than 8 A.M. on Monday.

Twenty-five years later, in 1988, Charlayne returned to the University of Georgia campus, this time as the first black person in the school's history to deliver the graduation speech.

Was the Montgomery bus boycott a success?

Not one black person rode on a Montgomery bus. The black community was so proud that they voted unanimously to continue the boycott and demand a fairer system of segregation on the buses: They wanted the bus company to let seated black passengers keep their seats for the whole ride.

A new young preacher named Martin Luther King Jr. was asked to be president of the strategy planning group, called the Montgomery Improvement Association. Information and instructions on car pools and walking were given during regular meetings held in churches and private homes.

But when the white city leaders refused to agree to the black community's demands, the black leaders filed a lawsuit in federal court charging that segregation on buses was unconstitutional. The white community retaliated by arresting the black leaders, using violence, and by other means, but the boycott continued. The boycott hurt not only the bus company, but other businesses in Montgomery. In the meantime, the cities of Richmond, Virginia; Little Rock, Arkansas; and Dallas, Texas; had ended segregation on their buses, which only made Montgomery, Alabama, look worse. Finally, on November 13, 1956, the U.S. Supreme Court ruled that Montgomery's segregated public transportation system was unconstitutional. The black community voted to call off the boycott, which had lasted for eleven months and eight days.

What happened to Rosa Parks after the Montgomery bus boycott?

Rosa Parks became a national figure and a hero in the black community. Already active in the NAACP and her church, she moved to Detroit in 1957 and later worked for Congressman John Conyers as a staff assistant. She received many awards and honorary degrees, and in 1987 founded the Rosa and Raymond Parks Institute of Self-Development, a career training center for black youth.

What is nonviolent resistance?

Nonviolent resistance (also called passive resistance) is a method of protest developed in the 1920s by an Indian

Satyagraha

Mohandas (Mahatma) Gandhi, an Indian leader of the 1920s, greatly influenced Martin Luther King. Gandhi's beliefs were central to Martin Luther King Jr.'s mode of protest.

Gandhi used the term *Satyagraha*, which meant "hold us to the truth," when explaining nonviolent resistance: "I discovered in the earliest stages that the pursuit of truth did not permit violence being inflicted on one's opponent, but that he must be weaned from error by sympathy."

Gandhi believed that by using nonviolent resistance, people could touch the hearts of their enemies, and thereby change them.

leader named Mohandas K. (Mahatma) Gandhi to fight against British colonial rule in India. Gandhi believed that people should not obey unfair laws, and should be willing to go to jail for disobeying those laws. While Gandhi believed that people should protest unfair treatment, he felt that they must never use violence. He called this method of protest "nonviolent resistance." By practicing these beliefs, Gandhi led his people in a successful revolution without resorting to violence. In 1947, using Gandhi's methods, the people of India, who had been ruled by England for many years, were able to become an independent country. Gandhi's methods were studied by Martin Luther King Jr. and other leaders, and used in the civil rights movement in the United States.

Did all African Americans believe in nonviolence?

There were some blacks who did not join in the peaceful activities because they did not believe in nonviolence. They would not take any insults, and vowed that they would fight back.

How did African Americans learn nonviolent resistance?

Nonviolence required compassion, commitment, courage, faith, and discipline. A group called the Fellowship of Reconciliation printed an illustrated pamphlet entitled *Martin Luther King, Jr. and the Montgomery Story* and distributed it throughout the South. It gave instructions on passive resistance. In workshops throughout the South, James Lawson, a young minister, helped Martin Luther King Jr. teach students and other activists how to use the tactic of passive resistance. The workshops demonstrated that nonviolence was not for the weak. Participants had to sit quietly while other students, pretending to be racists, jeered, poked, and spit at them.

What other events in the South led to black protest?

In 1955, the black community was shocked by the brutal murder of Emmett Till, a fourteen-year-old black Chicago boy. He was murdered in Mississippi by two white men, for "talking fresh" to a white woman. Emmett had been shot through the head and so badly beaten and mutilated that he was unrecognizable. To show the world what had happened to her son, his mother deliberately held an open-casket funeral. A photo of his mutilated body was shown in *Jet* magazine, and the entire country became angry at the monstrosity of the crime.

The two white men, Roy Bryant and J. W. Milem, were tried for murder. Mrs. Till made sure that black photographers, writers, and civil rights leaders attended the trial. Photographs and film of the trial were shown all over the country. For the first time, all Americans could see what was really happening in the South. They saw the pain of the Till family. They saw the hatred in the faces of the accused men and their families. They saw the all-white judge and jury. They also saw black people stand in a court of law and testify against white people.

As expected, however, the jury found the men not guilty, despite the evidence against them. People around the world condemned the racist verdict.

The anger, pain, and worldwide exposure resulting from Emmett Till's murder gave black people confidence that the world was watching the South. Emmett Till's mother was gratified at the support and shock that came from the publicity. She said, "If my son's death can mean something to the other unfortunate people all over the world, then for him to have died a hero would mean more than for him just to have died."

What was the Congress of Racial Equality?

The Congress of Racial Equality (CORE) was founded in Chicago in 1942 by James Farmer. Its goal was to confront racism and discrimination with direct action. CORE's first project was to desegregate a roller skating rink called White City on the South Side of Chicago. By 1944, CORE chapters had been formed in New York, Los Angeles, Philadelphia, Pittsburgh, and Detroit. During the 1960s, CORE used the **sit-in** method and went to the South to lead the **Freedom Rides.**

What were sit-ins?

Another unpleasant aspect of segregated life for African Americans in the South could be found at restaurants and lunch counters. In those days, blacks could only be served at counters that had signs reading COLORED ONLY. The success of the Montgomery bus boycott had made blacks more determined to break down segregation wherever it existed, and restaurants provided a good location to do it in a nonviolent manner.

On February 1, 1960, four black freshmen from North Carolina Agricultural and Technical College in Greensboro,

Police officers order black children in Birmingham, Alabama, to get into a van going to jail. The children were part of a huge civil rights demonstration in Birmingham on May 6, 1963.

North Carolina, decided to conduct just such a protest. Their names were Ezell Blair Jr., Franklin McCain, Joseph McNeil, and David Richmond. They had heard about African Americans demanding service at whites-only restaurants, and they knew that they could end up in jail for doing it themselves. But they talked each other into it, and the next day went to the Woolworth's on North Elm Street in Greensboro. They sat at the whites-only lunch counter, requested service, and refused to move until they got it. When nothing happened, they left at closing time and sought advice from a local dentist. He wrote to CORE, who sent a representative to organize more sit-ins by the students. Word spread, and a strategy was developed whereby enough students were recruited to stage daily sit-ins until segregation was defeated.

What kind of support did the students involved in the sit-ins receive?

Ella Baker, the executive director of the Southern Christian Leadership Conference (SCLC), was one of the organization's most militant members. She asked her colleagues at colleges and churches to help, and suggested that the SCLC call a meeting of students involved in the sit-ins. Three hundred students, black and white, attended. She advised them to form their own group, and the meeting ended with the formation of a student-run group that would organize the sit-in effort: the **Student Nonviolent Coordinating Committee (SNCC).**

What was the Southern Christian Leadership Conference?

The Southern Christian Leadership Conference (SCLC) was born of the Montgomery bus boycott. Founded in 1957, it consisted of black ministers from ten southern states. The group elected Martin Luther King Jr. as its president. It placed emphasis on legal action combined with nonviolent protest as the means to desegregate public transportation, public places, and public schools in America.

James Meredith

After serving nine years in the U.S. Air Force, James Meredith returned to his home state of Mississippi in 1960 and applied for admission to the University of Mississippi, the all-white university of the most racist state in the country. But Meredith was determined to attend, because of "a personal responsibility to change the status of my group." With his application, he enclosed a note informing the university that he was black. In response, he received a telegram advising him that applications received after January 25, 1961, were not being considered.

Unable to convince the admissions officers to look at his application him, Meredith filed a class action lawsuit charging that the rejection was based on his race. Constance Baker Motley, an attorney with the NAACP Legal Defense Fund, handled the suit. In September 1962, the U.S. Supreme Court ruled that Meredith should enter "Ole Miss." President Kennedy issued a proclamation that Meredith's entry not be blocked. The president also issued an executive order directing the secretary of defense to take steps to enforce the federal court's rulings.

By the night of Sunday, September 30, 1962, tension had mounted throughout the state. A large mob of angry whites, assuming that Meredith was inside, attacked the university's administration building with rocks, guns, and incendiary bombs and slashed the tires of the army trucks. Against these weapons, several hundred federal marshals, under orders not to use firearms, fought a losing battle employing only tear gas and nightsticks.

By the time it was over, a French reporter and a local repairman had been killed, and 160 marshals were injured. By dawn, armed federal troops arrived, and the campus grew quiet. That day, James Meredith registered, escorted by the chief U.S. marshal. When he went to his first class he was accompanied by U.S. marshals as well. Up to 20,000 troops were at one time stationed in and around the university, and their presence was still felt the next August when Meredith graduated in a peaceful ceremony.

What was the Student Nonviolent Coordinating Committee?

The Student Nonviolent Coordinating Committee (SNCC), often pronounced as "snick," was formed in 1960 to coordinate student protests, such as the sit-ins in the South. SNCC's goals were to desegregate public lunch

counters, rest rooms, parks, theaters, and schools; to register all blacks in the South to vote; and to get whites to practice nondiscriminatory practices in hiring.

In 1962, Robert Moses, a Harvard-educated school-
teacher, brought together a staff of SNCC organizers to help
black Mississippi citizens achieve voting rights.

What was the result of the sit-ins?

In many cases the students were attacked, beaten, and
arrested. The black community raised money to bail them
out. But the sit-ins attracted national publicity, and the students decided to keep up the pressure. By the end of
February 1960, sit-ins were being held in fifteen cities in a
number of states, including North Carolina, Virginia,
Florida, South Carolina, and Tennessee.

The first victory, a small one, came when blacks were
served at the Greyhound bus terminal in Nashville,
Tennessee. By May, six Nashville lunch counters began
serving blacks. By October, a month before the presidential
election, sit-ins had taken place in 112 southern cities, and
many were still going strong. On October 24, a truce was
called by Atlanta's city officials, merchants, and sit-in leaders. The sit-ins would stop, and any jailed protesters would
be released.

What were Freedom Rides?

Even though the Supreme Court had ruled that African
Americans had every right to sit anywhere they wanted to
on a bus, or to use bus terminal facilities without facing
segregation, when they tried to do so they were beaten,
thrown out, or jailed. In response to letters of complaint
CORE had received from these black bus riders, the members of SNCC decided to have an interracial group ride
buses through the South, which was what the Supreme
Court said they had the right to do. They wanted racists to
create a crisis so that the federal government would have to
enforce the law.

These Freedom Rides began on May 4, 1961, with thirteen passengers chosen and trained by CORE. Those who
rode were called Freedom Riders. The buses left Washington,
D.C., to travel through Virginia, North Carolina, and South

"We Shall Overcome"

During the civil rights movement, protest songs were often sung when participants gathered together and when mass demonstrations were being planned or held. People would grasp each other's hands, move from side to side, and sing these "freedom songs" as loud as they could.

Many of these songs came from nineteenth-century spirituals, but during the civil rights movement they were adapted to suit different circumstances. "We Shall Overcome" became an anthem of the movement:

We Shall Overcome,
we shall overcome,
we shall overcome,
someday.
Oh, deep in my heart,
I do believe, that
we shall overcome,
someday.

Carolina. They were scheduled to arrive in New Orleans on May 17, the anniversary of the 1954 *Brown v. Board of Education* decision.

What did the Freedom Rides accomplish?

On May 14, one of the buses was attacked by 200 angry people and then firebombed. A photograph of the burning bus covered the front pages of the nation's newspapers. In Birmingham, Alabama, riders of another bus were attacked by an angry mob. One of them was paralyzed for life. The violence against the Freedom Riders was given international press coverage. But the riders would not be stopped; whenever a group was attacked, another group of students would get on a bus and continue the Freedom Ride. After several more incidents and discussions with Attorney General Robert F. Kennedy and his representatives, pressure was placed on the bus company and the state governments to comply with federal law, and federal marshals were sent in to protect the riders.

How did blacks get voting rights?

After the murder of three voting rights organizers in 1964, the Mississippi Freedom Democratic Party, led by Fannie Lou Hamer, tried to unseat the all-white Mississippi delegation at the National Democratic convention later that year. Although unsuccessful, this demonstration brought public attention to the problem on national television, and eventually led to the passage of the Voting Rights Act of 1965, which abolished poll taxes and literacy tests.

Fannie Lou Hamer

Fannie Lou Hamer (1917–1977) was born a sharecropper and had just a few years of schooling, but she became a pivotal player in the civil rights movement.

In August 1964—when Democrats refused to allow African Americans to represent their party as delegates at the presidential convention—Fannie Lou Hamer led the Mississippi Freedom Democratic Party (MFDP) in their challenge against the all-white delegation. The MFDP felt that because Mississippi had such a large black population, there should certainly be black representation at the convention. Fannie Lou Hamer bravely testified to the committee that she had been jailed, beaten, and refused the right to vote. Many others risked their lives in this battle for fairness. The MFDP lost that year, but in 1968 she was among the first African American delegates to the Democratic National Convention.

She went on to speak often for the cause of civil rights.

How did the civil rights movement progress?

Between 1961 and 1963, over a million demonstrators protesting segregation, discrimination, and violence against blacks kept the pressure on in many southern cities. This wave of protests reached a peak during the spring of 1963, when federal troops were sent into Birmingham, Alabama, to stop racial violence. President John Kennedy reacted to the widespread demonstrations by introducing civil rights legislation designed to end segregation in public facilities.

What were Freedom Schools?

During the 1960s, many black children in the South worked in the fields instead of attending school, because school attendance was not required by law. In 1964, as part of a civil rights project called **Freedom Summer,** Freedom Schools were established to teach reading and math to black children in southern states. During Freedom Summer, community centers were opened that offered legal and medical help to poor blacks.

Septima Poinsette Clarke (1898–1987), a Tennessee educator, helped organize some of these schools, which were also known as citizenship schools. At these schools, African Americans were taught how to write, read, and stand up for their rights. They learned about the U.S. Constitution. They learned that "democracy" meant equal treatment for all people. They learned that one of the ways to make their voices heard was to vote. At that time, most southern blacks were not able to vote because they had to pass a literacy test before they could register. Septima Clarke taught her students how to pass this test at her citizenship schools. She traveled all over the South recruiting hundreds of teachers for these schools.

What political support did the civil rights movement get?

In 1958, black leaders met with President Dwight D. Eisenhower to request that he submit new civil rights legislation to Congress and openly pledge to support the *Brown v. Board of Education* decision. But like many Americans, President Eisenhower hadn't given much thought to black concerns and didn't consider them important. He did not address the black leaders' requests.

In 1960, the presidential election was hotly contested. The candidates were Richard M. Nixon, a Republican, and Senator John F. Kennedy, a Democrat. As the election approached, civil rights emerged as a major issue, but both candidates tried to avoid talking about it. If they were seen to be in favor of civil rights they might lose white votes. If they were against civil rights, they might lose black votes, which were growing thanks to voter registration drives. But when Martin Luther King Jr. was arrested during a demonstration and sentenced to four month's hard labor, John Kennedy made his first open civil rights move by calling Martin Luther King's wife with a promise to help. His brother, Robert Kennedy, followed with a call to the judge, who reversed the decision.

Without making an official endorsement, King publicly complimented Kennedy's courage and acknowledged that it helped get him released from jail. Receiving 75 percent of the black vote, John F. Kennedy won the election. African Americans had helped to make a president.

Johnson Publishing Company

When John H. Johnson (1918–) was in college in Chicago, he realized that there was no one publication with articles and information of interest to African Americans. He wondered if blacks would subscribe to such a magazine if he published it. Unable to get a bank loan, he borrowed $500 by using his mother's furniture as collateral. He sent a survey to 20,000 black insurance customers asking if they would subscribe to a magazine titled *Negro Digest: A Magazine of Negro Comment*. By October 1942, 3,000 people had sent in $2 subscriptions, and Johnson went ahead with his idea. The first issue was published in November 1942.

In 1945 Johnson began publishing a second magazine, *Ebony*, which used photos and original reporting to present black life and black achievements. Six years later, *Jet*, a weekly newsmagazine, was launched. *EM*, for *Ebony Man*, followed in 1985. Many of the African Americans profiled in Johnson's magazines were part of a growing black middle class. *Ebony, Jet*, and *EM* are still being published today.

How did blacks learn of the latest developments in the civil rights movement?

During the 1930s and 1940s, many local black newspapers had begun to publish national editions. By 1955 there were more than 200 black magazines and newspapers being published in the United States. Newspapers such as the *Chicago Defender*, the *Pittsburgh Courier*, and the *Baltimore Afro-American* and magazines such as *Jet* and *Ebony* reached black readers in every corner of the country. In 1955, New York's *Amsterdam News* was one of the most successful black newspapers in the country.

What resulted from the civil rights demonstrations?

President Kennedy felt that the country could no longer function with legal prejudice at its core. He appeared on national television to beg all Americans to eliminate segregation from the country. He stated that he would ask Congress to pass laws that would give all Americans the right to be served in public places such as

Martin Luther King Jr.

The Reverend Dr. Martin Luther King Jr. (1929–1968) was the most important civil rights leader of the 1960s. Using his belief in nonviolence, he helped to organize many peaceful marches, demonstrations, and boycotts. Through these actions, he helped African Americans win many rights that they had been denied for hundreds of years. His moving speeches and writings inspired other civil rights leaders.

At the March on Washington (1963) he delivered a speech that was broadcast all across the country. It was his most famous speech, called his "I Have A Dream" speech. In it, he said, "I have a dream today...that one day right there in Alabama, little black boys and black girls will be able to join hands with little white boys and girls as sisters and brothers. I have a dream today!"

In 1968, he was assassinated in Memphis, Tennessee. He was only thirty-nine years old.

hotels, restaurants, theaters, and stores. "No American in 1963 should have to endure denial of this right," he said.

As he promised, on June 19, 1963, President Kennedy delivered a new civil rights bill to Congress. It outlawed segregation in all interstate public accommodations and gave the U.S. attorney general power to start lawsuits for school integration. It also gave the attorney general the important power to cut off money to any federal programs in which discrimination occurred. It also contained a provision that helped ensure the right of black people to vote by declaring that a person who had a sixth grade education would be presumed to be literate.

What did the black leaders do to help President Kennedy's civil rights bill become a law?

Civil rights leaders had no intention of letting President Kennedy's bill die in Congress. To show how much the public wanted this law, they decided to have a demonstration in Washington, called the **March on Washington.** The goals of the march would be to demand passage of the Civil Rights Act, force integration of public schools by the end of the year, lobby for the enactment of a bill prohibiting job discrimination, and demand job training and placement for African Americans.

and so they became more violent. Bombs were left on the doorsteps of African American homes, and many who demonstrated or worked for the civil rights cause were injured, arrested, or even killed. Still, African Americans grew more confident; they continued to demonstrate, protesting and calling attention to the injustices of a racially divided society. They involved the president, requesting that he give them federal protection when they felt endangered. The media coverage also increased, allowing the rest of the country and the world to see what was going on in the South.

On November 22, 1963, after holding office for less than three years, President John F. Kennedy was shot and killed, and Vice President Lyndon Baines Johnson became the new president. President Johnson urged that Congress quickly pass the Civil Rights Bill in memory of the late president.

The Voting Rights Act was signed into law by President Johnson on August 6, 1965. This legislation had a dramatic impact on black voter registration, because it ended poll taxes, literacy tests, and other discriminatory practices. In Mississippi alone, the percentage of blacks registered to vote increased from 7 percent in 1964 to 59 percent in 1968.

The effects of the March on Washington did not end with federal legislation, however. President Johnson appointed the first black cabinet member, Secretary of Housing and Urban Development Robert C. Weaver, and the first black Supreme Court Justice, Thurgood Marshall, in 1967.

Black Power and Black Pride

What was the Black Power movement? ◆ What wa
[pp]ening in colleges? ◆ What was happening
[co]lleges? ◆ What did the Black Power supporter
[w]ant to achieve? ◆ What was life like in urban Black
communities in the 1960[s]? What did blacks do t
[ac]tively participate in conditions in the cities? ◆ Wh
[w]ere the Black Panthers? ◆ Who are the Black
[M]uslims? ◆ What role did black women have i
[po]litics after the Civil Rights Movement? ◆ Wha
[ot]her political gains did blacks attain in the 1960
[an]d 1970s? ◆ What progress resulted from th

What was the Black Power movement?

As the civil rights struggle continued into the 1960s, movements were created which used tactics and beliefs that differed from nonviolent resistance. Frustration with the police brutality that often resulted from peaceful demonstrations led civil rights workers like Stokely Carmichael, who worked with the Student Nonviolent Coordinating Committee (SNCC) in Alabama, to say they would never take a beating without hitting back. After being beaten and arrested in 1965, Carmichael spoke before a group of marchers who had been with him: "We been saying freedom for six years, and we ain't got nothin'. What we gonna start saying now is 'Black Power!'" The black power slogan was immediately adopted by the Congress of Racial Equity (CORE); along with the clenched fist, it became the symbol of young militants who didn't believe that nonviolence could achieve their civil rights goals. They were not willing to take the beatings anymore. They felt that black power would be achieved only when African Americans developed a more positive image of themselves.

What was happening in colleges?

Between 1970 and 1974 there was a 56-percent growth in black college enrollment. Black students began a movement to introduce black studies courses into college cur-

Wilma Rudolph

Wilma Rudolph, born in Tennessee in 1940, had scarlet fever and double pneumonia as a young child. She also contracted polio and couldn't walk without braces until she was eleven years of age.

Every day one of young Wilma's many brothers and sisters carefully massaged her crippled leg for her, until she was able to walk with the help of a corrective shoe. Eventually, however, Wilma started playing basketball and running; by the time she was sixteen years old, Wilma was breaking state basketball records for girls, and she was an undefeated sprinter for her high school track team.

When she ran track for Tennessee State University, she became renowned for her speed. She received much attention for her collegiate track performances, and in July 1960 she set a world record for the 200-meter dash.

In the 1960 Summer Olympics in Rome, Wilma Rudolph won three Olympic gold medals. She was the first American woman to do so.

Wilma Rudolph's example teaches a lesson about the merits of hard work, determination, bravery, and the love of family.

riculums. Some militant black students organized black student unions on college campuses and used tactics of disruption to demand black faculty members and black studies courses.

What was happening in sports?

In sports, 1960s black athletes brought a more individualistic style into college and professional sports, often making white coaches and sportswriters uncomfortable. For example, heavyweight boxer Muhammad Ali's refusal to be inducted into the army (in 1966) cost him his world championship, but also made him a hero to many blacks.

By 1968, blacks made up over half of all professional basketball players and almost a third of major league baseball and professional football players. That same year, Arthur Ashe (1943–1993) became the first black to win the U.S. Open men's singles tennis championship. At the 1968 Olympics in Mexico City, track and field medalists Tommie Smith (gold) and John Carlos (silver) gave the black power salute on the victory stand to protest racism in America—

and were subsequently suspended from the U.S. Olympic team. In December 1968, O. J. Simpson, running back for the University of Southern California, won college football's Heisman Trophy.

What did the Black Power supporters want to achieve?

Most Black Power supporters rejected the old civil rights strategies. They suggested a new strategy based on black control of the schools, stores, and other institutions in the black community. Some urged creation of separate black political parties. Others felt there should be a separate black state. But the main idea was to achieve black pride, black dignity, and black self-determination.

What was life like in urban black communities in the 1960s?

By the early 1960s, African Americans were frustrated by daily life in the cities. Black and other minority communities were called "inner cities." In these thickly populated slum areas, or **ghettos,** there were high crime rates, high unemployment, a lack of health services, poor garbage collection, overcrowding, discriminatory consumer practices, and police brutality.

What did blacks do to actively protest their conditions in the cities?

In the summer of 1964, black frustration in the ghettos began erupting in a series of riots that continued for four years. Almost every large city in the United States experienced similar rebellions. Primarily touched off by acts (or rumors) of police brutality, the most serious riots took place in New York's Harlem (1964), the Watts section of Los Angeles (1965), Newark, New Jersey (1967), and Detroit (1967). After the assassination of Martin Luther King Jr. in April 1968, riots, gunfire, burning, and looting broke out in 125 cities.

During these disturbances, neighborhoods burned down, people were injured and killed, and thousands were arrested. Many neighborhoods never recovered, remaining permanently burned-out and abandoned.

Police brutality against African Americans led Bobby Seale and Huey Newton to start the Black Panther Party in 1966.

Congress, that black women were allowed to serve their country and their constituencies in any substantial numbers.

What other political gains did blacks attain in the 1960s and 1970s?

In 1967, Thurgood Marshall (1908–1993) became the first black justice of the U.S. Supreme Court.

As the black residents of central-city areas became sizable minorities—and sometimes majorities—of the voting population, black candidates were able to win local elections. In 1967, Carl Stokes became the first black mayor of a major U.S. city, Cleveland, Ohio. Other black mayors followed: Richard Hatcher (Gary, Indiana), Thomas Bradley (Los Angeles, California), and Maynard Jackson (Atlanta, Georgia). Throughout the decade, black mayors were elected in Newark, New Jersey; Washington, D.C.; New Orleans, Louisiana; and other cities. By 1975, there were 135 black mayors in the United States. In 1975, there

Shirley Chisholm

Shirley Chisholm (1924–) was elected to the New York State legislature in 1964. With a degree in education, she had set up day care centers for working mothers in Brooklyn. The centers were so successful that Brooklyn residents elected her to the New York State legislature. In 1968, they elected her to Congress, where she was the first black congresswoman. She served for seven terms, from 1969 to 1982. In 1972, she decided to run for president and campaigned for the Democratic Party nomination. She lost the bid, but established a first for the women of America. She retired from Congress in 1982.

Black Women in Congress

Shirley Chisholm (New York), 1969–1982

Barbara Jordan (Texas), 1973–1979

Yvonne Braithwaite Burke (California), 1973–1979

Cardiss Collins (Illinois), 1973–

Katie Hall (Indiana), 1983–1985

Eleanor Holmes Norton (District of Columbia), 1991–

Maxine Waters (California), 1991–

Barbara-Rose Collins (Michigan), 1991–

Carol Moseley-Braun (Illinois), 1993–

Corinne Brown (Florida), 1993–

Carrie Meek (Florida), 1993–

Cynthia McKinney (Georgia), 1993–

Eva Clayton (North Carolina), 1992–

Eddie Bernice Johnson (Texas), 1993–

were 3,503 blacks holding elected offices in forty-five states, an increase of 88 percent since 1970.

African American legislators organized the Congressional Black Caucus in 1971, giving black U.S. representatives a way to address the needs of all minorities.

The National Black Political Convention, held in Gary, Indiana, in 1972, marked an effort to broaden black discussions of political alternatives. It was attended by 8,000 delegates.

In 1976, Andrew Young was appointed U.S. ambassador to the United Nations. Young thus became the highest-ranking black diplomat in the history of the United States and the first black ambassador to hold a cabinet-level position.

What progress resulted from the Black Power movement?

As a result of the actions of the 1960s, blacks made their biggest gains since slavery. Through the Affirmative Action and Equal Opportunity programs, qualified blacks were recruited by colleges and the job market. Reverend Jesse Jackson, a protégé of Martin Luther King Jr., founded People United to Save Humanity (PUSH), a black self-help group in 1971.

Barbara Jordan

Barbara Jordan (1936–1996) received her law degree in 1959 from Boston University. In 1966, she was elected to the Texas Senate, where she was the first black president pro tempore. She soon became known as an ardent promoter of civil rights for minorities and the poor.

In 1972, she was elected to the U.S. Congress, in the House of Representatives. In 1974, she was appointed to the House Judiciary Committee (along with another African American—John Conyers of Michigan) to help determine whether to impeach President Nixon for his unethical actions. It was then that she earned her reputation as a powerful speaker, condemning the president's role in the Watergate scandal.

She also delivered important and historic speeches at the 1976 and 1992 Democratic National Conventions and authored two books.

Rainbow Warrior

Jesse Jackson (1941–) is one of the most active civil rights leaders and a spokesman for all minorities in the United States.

Jackson was ordained a Baptist minister in 1968, when he had already become actively involved with the Southern Christian Leadership Conference (SCLC). In 1971, he left the SCLC to start his own organization—People United to Save Humanity (PUSH). Because of his persistence in combatting racism, his knowledge of certain issues, and his charismatic personality, Jackson became a highly visible leader of civil rights. His PUSH-EXCEL program, an offspring of PUSH, encouraged African American youth to excel academically.

In the 1980s he ran for president and received many votes for the Democratic nomination, although he failed to win the spot. He ran in 1984 and 1988 and made an impressive showing. His campaign was important because it demonstrated the important role that blacks played in national politics.

He remains engaged in political life, frequently acting as peacemaker in negotiations when racial troubles of any kind occur. His Rainbow Coalition, founded in 1984, promotes civil rights for all minorities. He also acts as an unofficial and at times controversial diplomat between the United States and other countries, traveling all over and meeting with foreign leaders. President Bill Clinton appointed him secretary of veteran affairs in 1993, the year he also received the Martin Luther King Jr. Nonviolent Peace Prize.

The number of blacks employed in better-paying white collar and skilled craftsmen occupations had increased from about 3 million in 1960 to about 5 million in 1971. In 1971, about 18 percent of young blacks were in college, compared to about 10 percent in 1965. In 1972 there were 2,264 black elected officials, 206 of them in state legislatures—more than double the 1964 figures. By the end of this period the 23 million African Americans had an annual income of more than $100 billion a year and constituted the second largest African community in the world.

What was everyday life like for blacks in the 1960s and 1970s?

By the beginning of the 1970s, blacks had suffered through forty years of disastrously high levels of unemployment, and large sectors of black America were locked into a state of almost permanent depression. Because of the closing of many factories and businesses, the employment situation of urban blacks in 1971 was worse than at any time since the Great Depression. Young black males had unemployment rates ranging between 40 and 50 percent. Under the impact of this situation and a national epidemic of hard drug use, the social structures of black America were changing: Unmarried mothers and broken homes were on the increase. Also contributing to this breakdown was a new white attitude: that America had done enough for blacks. During the administrations of Presidents Richard Nixon, Gerald Ford, Ronald Reagan, and George Bush, many civil rights gains, such as affirmative action, were threatened or discontinued.

What was the Black Arts Movement?

In the early 1960s, a major movement in American arts occurred. The Black Arts Movement, or **Black Aesthetic Movement,** was the largest African American cultural movement since the Harlem Renaissance.

All of the civil rights marches and the black pride and black power movements were closely linked to the exciting literature, poetry, and other writing of this movement. Some books published in the 1940s and 1950s greatly influenced this movement. Ralph Ellison's novel, *Invisible Man,* did much to bring black issues to the world's attention, and it won Ellison the National Book Award in 1952. This book

Invisible Man

Ralph Ellison (1914–1994) is a widely acclaimed literary figure. His only published novel, *Invisible Man,* has been praised as one of the twentieth century's most moving and extraordinary works.

The book shows how difficult life could be for an African American in the United States (the title refers to the lead character, a black man, who felt invisible in a white society). *Invisible Man* is meaningful to many readers because of its compassionate and vivid portrayal of what it feels like not to belong.

Ellison also wrote two collections of essays—*Shadows and Act* and *Going to the Territory.*

addressed the difficulties of being black in a white culture. Richard Wright's renowned novels addressed this issue as well.

The Black Arts Movement of the 1960s strived to create art that would have meaning for African Americans. The contributors to this era wanted to be wholly themselves, defining themselves honestly, frequently with fiery words and much emotion. Their work was often very political and nationalistic.

Amiri Baraka, a poet and essayist formerly known as Leroi Jones (1934–), was one of the leading artists in this movement.

The work from the Black Arts Movement continues to influence much American poetry and music today.

What was happening in popular music in the 1960s and 1970s?

There was a lot happening in the 1960s and 1970s! But first, it is important to understand what happened in the 1950s.

Evolving from blues, big-band swing, jazz, gospel, and other styles, **rhythm and blues** had a jumping, modern sound that appealed particularly to young audiences. This music began to take on many different shapes during the 1950s. Pianist and singer Ray Charles combined styles from jazz, blues, and gospel and released such classics as "What I'd Say" and "I Got a Woman." Fats Domino (1928–) created another sound influenced by the New Orleans style; his classics include "Ain't That a Shame" and "Blueberry Hill." Chuck Berry (1926–) combined some blues and country, started playing loud and fast guitar, and wrote about teenage life. He was one of the first people to play **rock 'n' roll,** and his songs, such as "Maybelleine" and "Johnny B. Goode" are now standards.

Meanwhile, other African Americans in the 1950s were singing and harmonizing gospel-like songs in small groups on street corners and trying to become a part of the new music scene. This music, known as **doo-wop,** became very successful, and groups like the Ravens, the Orioles, and the Dominoes become very popular. Gospel singers, such as Sam Cooke (1931–1964), started to perform popular vocal music.

Some Popular Black Musicians and Singers

Ray Charles (1932–). Singer and pianist. One of the most popular performers. Classics include "Georgia on My Mind," "Hit the Road, Jack," and "I Can't Stop Loving You." Inducted into the Rock 'n' Roll Hall of Fame in 1986, he was awarded a National Medal of the Arts in 1993.

Aretha Franklin (1942–). Singer and songwriter. Known as the the "Queen of Soul." Sings gospel, blues, and popular music. Most popular songs include "You Make Me Feel Like a Natural Woman," "Respect," "Chain of Fools," and "I've Never Loved a Man (The Way I Love You)".

Stevie Wonder (1950–). Pianist, singer, and composer. Performed as Little Stevie Wonder when he first signed with Motown. His single "Fingertips Part 2" went to number one on the charts when he was a twelve-year-old prodigy. Other hits include "For Once in My Life," "I Was Made to Love Her," "You Are the Sunshine of My Life," and "Superstition."

Otis Redding (1941–1967). Songwriter and singer. Hits include "These Arms of Mine," "Respect," and "Try a Little Tenderness." "Sittin' on the Dock of the Bay" became a gold record just a short time after he was killed in an airplane crash.

Diana Ross (1944–). Singer and actress. In the 1960s, as part of the Supremes, created such hits with the Motown label as "Baby Love," "You Can't Hurry Love," "Where Did Our Love Go?," and "Reflections." In 1970, she started her solo career and went on to win more commercial success with "Ain't No Mountain High Enough" and "Reach Out and Touch Somebody's Hand." Earned an Oscar nomination for her portrayal of Billie Holiday in *Lady Sings the Blues*. Had continued success in the 1980s and 1990s.

James Brown (1933–). Singer. Known as the "Godfather of Soul,"

All of this music from the 1950s was enormously influential to the **Motown** sound that emerged in the 1960s. The Motown Record Corporation, founded in 1959 by Berry Gordy, produced a distinctive sound that arose from blending rock 'n' roll with gospel and experimenting with sound techniques in the recording studio. Berry Gordy hired New York City's most talented musicians and songwriters to provide the musical accompaniment, and pop superstars were created. These stars included "girl groups" such as the Marvelettes, the Supremes, and Martha and the Vendellas; other groups such as Gladys Knight and the Pips, the Four Tops, the Temptations, and the Jackson Five;

and "Mr. Dynamite." Renowned for his live performances and energy. He and his band greatly influenced the evolution of funk. Hits include "Cold Sweat," "Sex Machine," and "I Got That Feeling." Inducted into the Rock 'n' Roll Hall of Fame in 1986.

Tina Turner (1939–). Singer and actress. As lead singer in the Ike and Tina Turner Revue, recorded the hit "River Deep, Mountain High." Solo career began in 1976. Won Grammy award for "What's Love Got to Do with It?" in 1985. Also appeared in *Tommy* and *Mad Max 3: Beyond the Thunderdome*. Continues to be popular in the 1990s.

Michael Jackson (1958–). Singer, dancer, actor, and composer. With the Jackson Five and produced by Motown, recorded hits such as "ABC," "I'll Be There," and "I Want You Back." During his solo career, he recorded *Off the Wall* (1979); *Thriller*, the best-selling album of all time; and

Bad. Won eight Grammys in 1984 for *Thriller*. His dancing, singing, and music videos continue to be popular in the 1990s.

Marvin Gaye (1939–1984). Singer and songwriter. Performed with the doo-wop group the Marquees, renamed the Moonglows. With Tammi Terrell, recorded hits "Your Precious Love" and "Ain't Nothing Like the Real Thing." During his solo career, recorded such hits as "Can I Get a Witness," "What's Going On," "Heard it Through the Grapevine," and "Mercy Mercy," and "Sexual Healing."

Al Green (1946–). Grammy-award-winning singer. Reverend Green sings gospel, soul, and popular music. Popular songs include "Let's Stay Together" and "Take Me to the River."

Sly and the Family Stone. Band. Recorded popular funk songs like "Everybody is a Star," "Thank You," "Hot Fun in the Summertime," and "Everyday People."

and singers including Stevie Wonder and Smokey Robinson. The Motown sound continues to have many, many listeners today.

Another style of music to emerge in the 1960s was soul. Soul, a mix of southern rhythm and blues styles and gospel vocalizations, is passionate and pulsing singing. James Brown is known as the "Godfather of Soul," and Aretha Franklin has been called the "Queen of Soul." Other popular soul singers include Curtis Mayfield (1942–) and Otis Redding.

Rock guitarist Jimi Hendrix (1942–1970) was a pioneering rock musician. He revolutionized the role of the electric guitar; his hits include "All Along the Watchtower," "Foxy Lady," and "Hey Joe."

By the late 1970s, there were many popular African American funk, rap, dance, and rock musicians.

What is affirmative action?

In 1972, Congress passed two laws: the Equal Employment Opportunity (EEO) Act and the Equal Opportunity Act. These two laws helped to force open job opportunities for all Americans. Referred to as the affirmative action bills, they required most federal agencies, state governments, public institutions, and local governments to hire more blacks, women, and other Americans who had been excluded from many jobs because of discrimination.

Government agencies and private companies that received government funds were required to purchase a percentage of goods and services from black-, female-, and minority-owned companies. Because of affirmative action, and the willingness of more people to fight for their right to a good job, there has been a significant increase in the number of African Americans, women, and other minorities in all areas of employment. There has also been a growth in the number of successful businesses owned by these groups.

Was affirmative action a success?

While it resulted in enormous professional progress for African Americans, affirmative action has come under attack in recent years. Some critics believe it is no longer needed, and that job discrimination does not exist anymore. They also believe that the quota system, one of the methods used under affirmative action to help open the doors of employment for all Americans, is **reverse discrimination.** The quota system essentially sets aside a certain number of positions within a company for a particular group that has been discriminated against. Critics feel this system denies jobs to white males who are sometimes more qualified for the jobs.

Supporters believe that affirmative action is still necessary, and without it companies will no longer feel obligated to ensure job opportunities for all Americans. Some people feel that minorities won't be hired and promoted on a fair and equal basis without some kind of forceful government regulation.

Did all civil rights advances come from demonstrations?

Not all of the civil rights movement took place in the streets and at lunch counters. Many changes and advances came about after years of working quietly behind the scenes.

By the mid-1960s, minorities were becoming more aware of themselves and of their potential. However, there were few black history materials that portrayed the black experience accurately and completely. Although schools were integrated, textbooks and courses did not discuss the contributions of African Americans, women, and other minorities. Teachers, parents, and students began expressing their concern about the lack of good cultural materials.

Through persistence, school districts were convinced that a multicultural education was the best approach, and cultural diversity was a strength, not a liability. School administrators passed their needs and concerns on to publishers and universities which, in turn, began publishing better materials and making multicultural education courses a part of teacher certification. That process took years, and continues today.

The media was another target of awareness groups. Television had no programs with regular African American, Asian, or Hispanic stars. Commercials stereotyped women and excluded minority consumers. Slowly, nonwhite faces began to appear in television shows and movies.

In 1978, the U.S. Postal Service, in response to challenges from African Americans to honor the accomplishments of blacks, began issuing the Black Heritage postage stamp series. Over the years, the series honored black figures including Harriet Tubman, Martin Luther King Jr., and W. E. B. Du Bois.

How did Black History Month begin?

A leading black scholar, Carter G. Woodson, (1875–1950) was concerned that books written about African

Americans were inaccurate and racist. Many of the history books that were written during his lifetime did not mention the cultural contributions of African Americans. As a result, in 1915 Woodson organized the Association for the Study of Negro Life and History. Some of the books he wrote include *The Education of the Negro Prior to 1861, A Century of Negro Migration* (1915), *The Negro in Our History* (1922), and *The History of the Negro Church.*

In 1927, Woodson began the observance of a Negro History Week to help make information available to the public about African American history. He was a cofounder of the *Negro History Bulletin,* a journal that published black scholarly research about African Americans. In 1976, Woodson's Negro History Week was expanded to Black History Month, which is still celebrated every year in February.

What political gains did blacks attain in the 1980s and 1990s?

In the 1980s, black mayors were elected in Chicago, Philadelphia, New York City, and other cities throughout the country. By 1990, there were 318 black mayors.

In 1983 and 1988, Jesse Jackson declared his candidacy for the Democratic presidential nomination and promised to create a "rainbow coalition" of support among poor and dispossessed Americans. Although unsuccessful in this bid, he was the second black presidential candidate to campaign for nomination by a major political party. In 1989, General Colin L. Powell became chairman of the Joint Chiefs of Staff, the country's top military position. He was the first African American to hold this position.

By late 1990, there were 7,480 black elected officials in the United States, including twenty-six members of Congress. In 1991, federal judge Clarence Thomas was appointed a U.S. Supreme Court justice. His appointment followed a nationally televised Senate Judiciary Committee investigation into charges that he sexually harassed his assistant, Anita Hill, ten years previously.

Publications Reporting on Black Life

American Legacy (Rodney J. Reynolds, publisher)

Black Enterprise (Earl G. Graves, publisher)

Ebony (John H. Johnson, publisher)

Emerge (Debra L. Lee, publisher)

Essence (Edward Lewis, publisher)

Jet (John H. Johnson, publisher)

Famous Amos

Wally Amos (1937–) started working for The William Morris Agency—a very successful and profitable talent agency—as a mail clerk. Eventually, he became the first African American talent agent for the agency. Amos discovered many successful acts, including Simon & Garfunkel, a folk-rock singing duo. He also represented such stars as The Temptations, Patti Labelle, and Marvin Gaye.

In 1975, Amos started something entirely different—a chocolate chip cookie empire! By 1980, Famous Amos Chocolate Chip Cookies were truly famous. The company sold more than 5 million dollars' worth of cookies each year. In 1980 he also donated one of his trademark panama hats to The National Museum of American History.

Colin Powell

Colin Powell, born in New York City in 1937, is one of the most admired African Americans in the country today.

His long career in the military began when he was in college. While at City College of New York, Powell was part of the Reserve Officer Training Corp (ROTC) Program. Upon graduation from college in 1956, Powell became a second lieutenant for the U.S. Army. In 1962, he was an adviser for the U.S. Forces in Vietnam.

He climbed up the military ladder quickly, becoming assistant division commander in 1981. Colin Powell was appointed National Security Adviser by President Ronald Reagan in 1987, and, in 1989, he achieved the highest military post in the United States—chairman of the Joint Chiefs of Staff.

In 1991, Powell became renowned all over the world for his leadership during the Persian Gulf War.

In 1992, Arkansas governor Bill Clinton ran for president with record-breaking levels of black support; when he won, he filled his cabinet and administration with blacks, including Secretary of Commerce Ronald Brown, Secretary of Agriculture Mike Espy, Secretary of Energy Hazel O'Leary, and Secretary of Veterans Affairs Jesse Brown. In the months that followed, blacks reversed some of the policies of the Reagan-Bush years.

In 1992, the first black woman senator, Carol E. Moseley-Braun, was elected from Illinois.

Did people forget about the laws passed during the civil rights movement?

Americans did not forget about the laws passed during the civil rights movement; there were some new gains made in the 1980s and 1990s. In 1982, both houses of Congress voted to extend the Voting Rights Act of 1965 for twenty-five years.

In 1983, President Ronald Reagan signed a bill establishing Martin Luther King Day as a federal holiday. It was first celebrated as a federal holiday on January 20, 1986.

In 1983, some 250,000 marchers came together in Washington, D.C., to commemorate the twentieth anniversary of the historic March on Washington.

In 1985 and 1986, the Supreme Court upheld state affirmative action plans to grant special employment preferences to minorities. In 1995, however, the Supreme Court reversed its position on the constitutionality of affirmative

women and minorities to use the courts to fight discrimination in hiring or on the job. President George Bush signed the Civil Rights Act of 1991, which limited affirmative action.

What were race relations like?

Racism persisted in communities, companies, law enforcement, and sports. Lawsuits and civil disturbances showed just how prevalent racism remained. Racial disturbances occurred in 1991 in Crown Heights, Brooklyn, after a car transporting a Hasidic rabbi was involved in an accident in which a black child was killed. Angry residents reacted in three nights of rioting, during which a twenty-nine-year-old Australian rabbinical scholar was stabbed to death.

In Los Angeles, a citizen's videotape captured the 1991 beating of Rodney King, a black motorist, by four white policemen. The acquittal of the officers in 1992 resulted in riots in inner city Los Angeles that were the most destructive in American history.

Corporations such as Texaco and Denny's were sued, or threatened with lawsuits, for racist treatment of cus-

The Films of Spike Lee

In the 1980s, an exciting and dynamic filmmaker named Spike Lee (1957–) began to gain attention for his innovative work. Lee, an African American, creates films that portray black lives and perspectives that much of America has rarely seen before. Many of his movies have been daring, frequently generating controversy. But his characters are consistently lively, real, and compassionate. Lee's films are also exceptional for his unconventional camera angles, bright and bold colors, lively pacing, and other exciting cinematic techniques.

His first widely released movies were She's Gotta Have It (1986) and School Daze (1988). Do The Right Thing (1989) brought him the acclaim he sought; it was very popular, and critically and commercially successful.

Jungle Fever (1991) explored an interracial relationship, and Malcolm X (1992) opened many young people's eyes to the life and teachings of the 1960s black leader. The movie renewed interest in this extremely popular figure. In 1997, Lee made a documentary, Four Girls, about the four young schoolgirls who were killed in 1963 when a church in Alabama was bombed.

tomers and/or employees, and made legal settlements to those harmed.

What did people do to fight racism?

Many companies, communities, schools, and other institutions made special efforts to hire staffs of all racial backgrounds and to teach subjects on many cultures in the schools. The words used to define these became a part of everyday vocabulary: tolerance, diversity, and multiculturalism. Minority consumers demanded to see people who looked like them in advertising, on television, and in movies.

At the Million Man March, speeches were made by such people as poet Maya Angelou, Jesse Jackson, and Rosa Parks.

In 1996, the controversial Minister Louis Farrakhan, in an attempt to urge black men to take responsibility for their own lives and fight racism, drugs, violence, and unemployment, called for a million black men to travel to Washington, D.C. This all-day event, which took place on October 16, was called the **Million Man March.** Its supporters included mayors, ministers, and several black members of Congress.

What gains were made to recognize blacks in everyday life?

There was an increased coverage of the black perspectives in mainstream culture. Black actors were seen more

Black Role Models in the 1980s and 1990s

Mae C. Jemison. The first black woman to become a U.S. astronaut, she flew into space as a member of the crew of the space shuttle *Endeavor* in 1992.

Toni Morrison. In 1983, she became the first black woman novelist to win a Pulitzer Prize, which was awarded to her for her novel *Beloved*; in 1993, Morrison became the first African American to win the Nobel Prize in literature.

Robert C. Maynard. He bought the *Oakland Tribune* in 1983 for $22 million, becoming the first black owner of a major mainstream daily newspaper.

Michael Jordan. The Chicago Bulls superstar won his sixth consecutive National Basketball Association scoring title in 1992; by the end of the 1996–97 season, he had won the scoring title nine times in all.

Tiger Woods. In 1997, this twenty-one-year-old became the youngest person—and the first person of African descent—to win the Masters golf championship.

Some Black Women Writers

Maya Angelou (1928–). Poet and novelist. Works include her autobiographical *I Know Why the Caged Bird Sings* (1970) and *The Heart of a Woman* (1981), the novels *All God's Children Need Traveling Shoes* (1986) and *Wouldn't Take Nothing for My Journey Now*. Read her poem "On the Pulse of Morning" during President Bill Clinton's inauguration in 1993.

Alice Walker (1944–). Poet, novelist, essayist, and children's book writer. Works include novel *The Color Purple* (1982), which won the Pulitzer Prize for fiction; *The Temple of My Familiar* (1989); *Possessing the Secret of Joy* (1992); poetry collections *Once* (1968) and *Revolutionary Petunias and Other Poems* (1973), a National Book Award nominee; and *In Love & Trouble: Stories of Black Women* (1973), winner of the Rosenthal Award.

Terry McMillan (1951–). Novelist. Works include *Mama* (1987) and *Disappearing Acts* (1989). *Waiting to Exhale* (1992) was a best-selling novel that became a successful movie. *How Stella Got Her Groove Back* (1996) was also a nationwide best-seller.

Gloria Naylor (1950–). Novelist. *The Women of Brewster Place* (1983) won the American Book Award, and was made into a movie for television in 1988. Other novels include *Linden Hills* (1985), *Mama Day* (1988), and *Bailey's Cafe* (1993).

frequently on television and in movies. The young black film directors Spike Lee, Robert Townsend, and John Singleton made films that showed the black experience. They also hired blacks and gave them opportunities in the industry.

Rap music, which was created by young blacks who lived in the cities, told of daily life as a black youth and gained a huge following, among both black and white youths.

Magazines specially targeted to black readers reported on black accomplishments, continuing a trend started by John H. Johnson's *Ebony*.

A new generation of writers, such as Terry McMillan, Connie Briscoe, and Bebe Moore Campbell, told about the lives and relationships of black women, revealing a huge market for such works. Children's books, both fiction and nonfiction, depicted blacks and other minorities as fully realized characters, and told of the history of blacks and other minorities so that the coming generations would be aware of those who had come before them.

GLOSSARY

A

abolitionists people who fought to end slavery

American Colonization Society group of white abolitionists formed in 1860 to help African Americans return to Africa

B

Black Aesthetic Movement artistic movement of the 1960s in which African Americans aimed to create art and literature that would be meaningful to all blacks

Black Codes laws that limited the rights of African Americans. Most were enacted after the Civil War

Black Panther Party militant organization founded in 1966 that condemned discrimination, capitalism, and the white power structure in general; condoned the use of violence to promote their message

Buffalo Soldiers name given by Native Americans to the African Americans of the Ninth and Tenth Regiments who were sent west to battle outlaws and Native Americans in the mid-1800s

C

civil rights rights of all citizens to legal, social, and economic equality and protection under the law

colony settlement started by a government outside its own borders, usually on land not formally claimed by another nation

Compromise of 1850 the Congressional agreement that abolished slavery in Washington, D.C.; proclaimed California a free state; gave New Mexico and Utah the right to decide for themselves whether they wanted slavery; and enacted the Fugitive Slave Act

Compromise of 1877 the Congressional agreement between Rutherford Hayes's Republicans and southern Democrats that enabled white majorities to regain control of state governments in the South; blacks were left unprotected from discrimination and persecution

Confederacy the rebel Southern states that broke away from the United States and fought against the Union in the Civil War

Continental army   colonists who fought the British during the Revolutionary War

D

discrimination   the practice of treating a person or persons differently because they belong to a race, religion, class, or group different from that of the discriminator

doo-wop   type of vocal music that consists of several harmonies, unaccompanied by instruments; popularized by street-corner singing groups in the 1950s

E

exodusters   the hundreds of blacks who left the South and headed west to Kansas, Missouri, Iowa, and Nebraska after Reconstruction

F

field hands   slaves who worked in the fields; also called field slaves

fraternity   social organization of male college or university students and alumni

Freedmen's Bureau   program created by the U.S. War Department to assist freed slaves; provided educational and health services, food, and clothing

Freedom Rides   system arranged by Student Nonviolent Coordinating Committee, in 1961, in which groups of blacks and whites rode buses together through the South; designed to draw federal attention so blacks could ride southern buses safely

Freedom Summer   civil rights project of summer of 1964, when blacks and whites took part in the voter registration project in Mississippi; Freedom Schools and community centers were also established

G

ghettos   heavily populated poor areas, mostly inhabited by minority groups

H

Harlem Renaissance   Harlem-centered period, begun in the 1920s, when black creative expression flowered

K

Ku Klux Klan   secret white organization formed in 1865 to suppress African Americans who exercised their new rights

L

literacy tests   discriminatory tests given by some southern states to blacks. Blacks were required to pass such tests before they were allowed to vote; whites did not have to take the tests.

lynching   the murder of an individual, usually by hanging or burning, by a mob

M

March on Washington   massive demonstration organized by black civil rights leaders in 1963 to show Congress and President Kennedy how much the public supported the proposed civil rights law

Middle Passage   the long, difficult shipboard passage across the Atlantic, from Africa to North America, the middle part of a slave ship's three-part trip

Million Man March   all-day event organized by Minister Louis Farrakhan in 1996. The purpose was to urge black men to take responsibility for their lives and to fight violence, drugs, and racism

Montgomery bus boycott   the mass refusal of blacks in Montgomery, Alabama, in 1955 to ride buses to protest discriminatory practices on their public transportation system

Motown   record company founded by Berry Gordy that created a distinctive and extremely popular music style in the 1960s

N

NAACP   organization founded in 1909 to promote equality and justice for African Americans

New Deal   program designed by Franklin Delano Roosevelt to help country recover after the Great Depression; included several social and relief programs and important legislation

P

plantations   large farms or estates where a crop such as cotton, tobacco, rice, or sugar was cultivated, usually by slaves

poll taxes   discriminatory taxes that blacks were required to pay if they wanted to vote

R

Reconstruction   the period between 1865 and 1877 when the United States was reorganized after the Civil War. During this period, several laws were passed to protect the rights of all free people in the United States.

Return to Africa   a movement begun in the early 1800s that was led by free blacks, politicians, and abolitionists who felt that the problem of slavery would be solved by sending blacks back to Africa

reverse discrimination   form of discrimination in which the group who traditionally holds power is treated unfairly

rhythm and blues   type of popular music that developed from several other African American, folk-based styles; eventually evolved into rock 'n' roll

rock 'n' roll   style of music characterized by a catchy, heavily accented beat; it emerged from folk, blues, and rhythm and blues

S

secede   to break away from

segregation   the practice of separating people by race, ethnicity, or religion

sharecropping   process by which poor blacks and white farmers sold their labor for a share of the crop they produced rather than for cash

sit-in   practice by which blacks sat at white-only lunch counters and refused to move until they received service

SNCC   an acronym for the Student Nonviolent Coordinating Committee, an organization, founded in 1960, made up of black and white students who worked together to fight racial discrimination

states' rights   the rights held by states to regulate matters within their own borders as long as the state's laws are not contrary to the Constitution; the concept was used by Southern states to uphold Black Codes

U

Underground Railroad   the system of houses and people that illegally helped runaway slaves reach safety in the North or Canada; also called the Liberty Line

Union   the Northern States that fought against the Confederacy in the Civil War

W

white supremacy   philosophy that whites are superior to other races

WPA   an acronym for the Works Progress Administration, a program of the New Deal that employed about 3 million people a year on public works projects

BIBLIOGRAPHY

Adero, Malaika, ed. *Up South: Stories, Studies and Letters of this Century's African-American Migrations*. New York: New Press, 1993.

African Americans: Voices of Triumph: Leadership. Virginia: Time-Life Books, 1994.

African Americans: Voices of Triumph: Perseverance. Virginia: Time-Life Books, 1994.

Bennett, Lerone Jr. *Before the Mayflower: A History of Black America*, 6th ed. New York: Penguin Books, 1993.

Clay, William L. *Just Permanent Interests: Black Americans in Congress, 1870–1991*. New York: Amistad Press, 1992.

Cook, Janet and Stephen Kirby. *Introduction to Politics & Governments*. London: Usborne Publishing, 1986.

Cowan, Tom and Jack Maguire. *Timelines of African American History*. New York: Perigee Books, 1994.

Dennis, Denise. *Black History for Beginners*. New York: Writers and Readers, 1984.

Driskell, David, David Levering Lewis, and Deborah Willis Ryan. *Harlem Renaissance Art of Black America*. New York: Harry Abrams, 1994.

Du Bois, W. E. Burghardt. *The Negro*. New York: Henry Holt & Company, 1915.

Franklin, John Hope. *From Slavery to Freedom: A History of Negro Americans*, 4th ed. New York: Alfred A. Knopf, 1974.

Hudson, Wade and Valerie Wilson Wesley. *Afro-Bets Book of Black Heroes from A to Z*. New Jersey: Just Us Books, 1988.

Huggins, Nathan Irvin. *Harlem Renaissance*. New York: Oxford University Press, 1973.

Igus, Toyomi, Veronica Freeman Ellis, Diane Patrick, and Valerie Wilson Wesley. *Book of Black Heroes, Volume 2: Great Women In The Struggle*. New Jersey: Just Us Books, 1991.

Johnson, Jacqueline. *Stokely Carmichael: The Story of Black Power*. New Jersey: Silver Burdett Press, 1990.

Kellogg, William O. *American History the Easy Way*, 2d. ed. New York: Barron's Educational Series, Inc., 1995.

Lerner, Gerda, ed. *Black Women in White America: A Documentary History*. New York: Vintage Books, 1972.

Lynch, Hollis R. *The Black Urban Condition*. New York: Thomas Y. Crowell Company, 1973.

McKissack, Patricia and Fredrick McKissack. *The Civil Rights Movement in America From 1865 to the Present*, 2nd ed. Chicago: Childrens Press, 1987.

Myers, Walter Dean. *Now Is Your Time: The African-American Struggle for Freedom*. New York: HarperCollins, 1991.

Patrick, Diane. *The Executive Branch*. New York: Franklin Watts, 1994.

Ploski, Harry A. and James Williams. *The Negro Almanac*. New York: John Wiley & Sons, 1983.

Quarles, Benjamin. *The Negro in the Making of America*. New York: Collier Books, 1969.

Rees, Bob and Marika Sherwood. *The Black Experience*. New York: Peter Bedrick Books, 1993.

Steck-Vaughn Social Studies: *Our Country's History*. Texas: Steck-Vaughn Company, 1991.

Trotter, Joe William Jr. *From A Raw Deal to A New Deal? African Americans 1929–1945*. New York: Oxford University Press, 1996.

Williams, Juan. *Eyes on the Prize: America's Civil Rights Years, 1954–1965*. New York: Viking Penguin, 1987.

THE NEW YORK PUBLIC LIBRARY'S RECOMMENDED READING LIST

African American Voices of Triumph: Creative Fire. Alexandria, VA: Time-Life Books, 1994.

African American Voices of Triumph: Perseverance. Alexandria, VA: Time-Life Books, 1994.

Brown, Kevin. *Malcolm X*. Danbury, CT: Millbrook, 1995.

Cooper, Michael L. *Bound for the Promised Land*. NY: Lodestar, 1995.

Copage, Eric V. *A Kwanzaa Fable*. NY: Morrow, 1995.

Cottman, Michael H. *Million Man March*. NY: Crown, 1995.

Curry, Constance. *Silver Rights*. Chapel Hill, NC: Algonquin, 1995.

Davis, Francis, ed. *The History of the Blues*. NY: Hyperion, 1995.

Feelings, Tom. *The Middle Passage*. NY: Dial, 1995.

Frank, Andrew. *The Birth of Black America: The Age of Discovery and the Slave Trade:* Philadelphia, PA: Chelsea House, 1996.

Garrity, John. *Tiger Woods*. NY: Simon & Schuster, 1997.

Harrington, Geri. *Jackie Joyner-Kersee*. NY: Chelsea House, 1995.

Haskins, James. *Black Dance in America*. NY: Crowell, 1990.

——. *The Harlem Renaissance*. Danbury, CT: Millbrook, 1997.

hooks, bell. Bone Black. NY: Holt, 1996

Jeffery, Laura S. *Barbara Jordan*. Springfield, NJ: Enslow, 1997.

Johnson, Venice, ed. *Heart Full of Grace*. NY: Simon & Schuster, 1995.

Jones, K. Maurice. *Say It Loud: The Story of Rap Music*. Danbury, CT: Millbrook, 1994.

Katz, William Loren. *The Black West*, 3rd Edition. NY: Touchstone, 1996..

Kelley, Robin D. G. *Into the Fire*. NY: Oxford University Press, 1996.

King, Martin Luther, Jr. *I Have a Dream*. San Francisco, CA: HarperSanFrancisco, 1983.

Levine, Ellen. *Freedom's Children*. NY: Putnam, 1992.

McKissack, Patricia C. and Frederick McKissack, Jr.. *Black Diamond*. NY: Scholastic, 1994.

———. *Rebels Against Slavery*. NY: Scholastic, 1995.

Meltzer, Milton. *Frederick Douglass: In His Own Words*. San Diego, CA: Harcourt Brace, 1995.

Myers, Walter Dean. *Malcolm X: By Any Means Necessary*. NY: Scholastic, 1993.

———. *One More River to Cross*. San Diego, CA: Harcourt Brace, 1996.

Osofsky, Audrey. *Free to Dream*. NY: Lothrop, Lee & Shepard, 1996.

Patterson, Lillie. *A. Philip Randolph*. NY: Facts on File, 1995.

Rappoport, Ken. *Bobby Bonilla*. NY: Walker, 1993.

———. *Shaquille O'Neal*. NY: Walker, 1994.

Reef, Catherine. *Black Explorers*. NY: Facts on File, 1996.

Rennert, R. S. *African American Answer Book: Sports*. NY: Chelsea House, 1995.

Rinaldi, Ann. *Hang a Thousand Trees with Ribbons*. San Diego, CA: Harcourt Brace, 1996.

Schulke, Flip. *He Had a Dream*. NY: Norton, 1994.

Schuman, Michael. *Martin Luther King*. Springfield, NJ: Enslow, 1996.

Sexton, Adam. *Rap on Rap,* NY: Delta, 1995.

Silverman, Jerry. *Just Listen to this Song I'm Singing*. Danbury, CT: Millbrook, 1996.

Smith, John D. *Black Voices from Reconstruction*. Danbury, CT: Millbrook, 1996.

Terry, Roderick. *One Million Strong*. Edgewood, MD: Duncan & Duncan, 1996.

Thornton, Yvonne S. *The Ditchdigger's Daughters*. NY: Birch Lane, 1995.

Whitelaw, Nancy. *Mr. Civil Rights*. Greensboro, NC: Morgan Reynolds, 1995.

Wilker, Josh. *Julius Irving*. Philadelphia, PA: Chelsea House, 1997.

———. *The Harlem Globetrotters*. Philadelphia, PA: Chelsea House, 1997.

Woods, Paula L. and Felix H. Liddell, eds. *I Hear a Symphony*. NY: Anchor, 1995.

Woodson, Jacqueline, ed. *A Way Out of No Way*. NY: Holt, 1996.